OUT OF EGYPT: VOLUME I

A KID FROM BENI SUEF

DR. ELHAMY KHALIL

To my wife Samia and my two sons Michael, John and their families,
who encouraged me to write my memoir.

To the institutions and people in Beni Suef, who shaped my character.

And to the people of Egypt, who gave me the opportunity
for success and enriched my life.

Contents

Chapter 1
MY EARLY CHILDHOOD

Egypt, the land of my birth, is the gift of the Nile. This magnificent river, the longest in the world, flows south to north for more than 700 miles through Egypt, providing lush, fertile fields in its valleys for the cities, towns, and villages that have sprung up since ancient times. My hometown, Beni Suef, is seventy miles south of Cairo. Situated on the west side of the Nile, it comprises only nine square miles that people could walk through from one end to the other in an hour. Our city was nevertheless the capital of the province of Beni Suef, yet vastly different from the teeming masses that inhabit Egypt's capital, Cairo.

Beni Suef was a relatively quiet city when I was growing up there. We had no need for traffic lights or rules because back then we had no buses or other form of public transportation. Not even the few wealthy people owned cars. But one thing all Egyptian communities had in common was the Muslim command to pray five times a day: "As-salatu khairon-min-an-naum!" "Prayer is better than sleep!"

In the early dawn hours of October 23rd 1935, as the muezzin was calling Muslims to prayer from the top of a Beni Suef minaret, a woman was suffering loudly from labor pains. Neighbors looked through their windows to see from which house the cries were coming. On our small street everyone knew who was pregnant and how far along they were in their pregnancy. Apparently it was too early for any of them to deliver.

However, my mother, Dawlat Ibrahim, was ready to give birth. My father rushed to get the neighborhood midwife, Om Ali, (the mother of Ali). An

1

hour later Om Ali announced gleefully that the baby was a boy. There was joy not only that the delivery was uneventful but also that the baby was a male. In Egypt in those days boys were preferred to girls. It meant that the family name would continue and there would be a man in the house in case the father died early in life, which was common before the days of antibiotics.

A first-born boy changed the name that people, other than immediate family, called his mother. From that day on she would be called Om (mother). My mother was now Om Elhamy, mother of Elhamy, my given name.

My father was overjoyed. I was his third son, the first from his second wife. I came at the right time in his life. The previous few years had been hard on him financially as the price of cotton plummeted with the Great Depression of 1929. His income from the land that his family owned decreased so much that he was unable to pay the teachers of the private school that he part-owned, especially with the lower student enrollment. In 1932 he had to sell my mother's jewelry to keep the school going. During the summer of 1935, a month before I was born, his school and the Coptic school merged, ensuring the survival of both. In addition, the price of cotton was starting to rebound. My father called me his "good luck son."

My older half-sister, Hend, who was later to become a nurse-midwife, told me that I was so tiny my head was no larger than a tennis ball! I must have been born prematurely but back then there was no weighing or measuring of a newborn at home. Nor were those details recorded on the birth certificates which were usually registered one to two weeks after birth.

Small as I was, I was told later that I was a bundle of energy. I walked at ten months and by my second year I was talking non-stop. My mother said that she got tired just watching me move around, hoping that I wouldn't get into any mischief or get injured. She was right to worry. At age two I was standing by a door when a sudden wind slammed it shut on my right foot. My big toe started to bleed and swelled up. After a few weeks, the nail fell off. The new nail grew in deformed, splitting into two pieces shaped like a pyramid. The nail is still split to this day. It makes putting on a sock on that foot difficult as it often gets tangled in the broken nail.

In another incident, also at the age of two, I poked my head between two of the iron rods in the balcony railing but I couldn't pull it back. I screamed. My mother, nursing my younger sister on her lap, came running and somehow squeezed my head free. She told me if this happened again they

2

may have to cut one of my ears off. I was mortified, as well as scared. Never again.

Just eight months later, during the summer of 1938, we were visiting my maternal grandmother in Cairo. My mom was holding my hand standing on a curb waiting for the traffic to pass so we could cross the road. In those days people didn't have the right of way, even on busy streets. I looked around and saw there was only one car coming and it was far away. I thought that being a fast runner I could easily get across the street. I slipped my hand from my mother's and started running towards the opposite curb. I obviously underestimated my speed versus the car's speed.

Suddenly, I was in the middle of the road and the car was almost upon me. Luckily, the driver saw me and slammed on the brakes so hard that the car came to a screeching halt just a few feet from me. I was terrified. I stumbled and fell. Next, I remember two men carrying me to a pharmacy across the street to be checked for injuries. I wasn't hurt but the memory of that mishap is etched into my brain. On the way home I was totally and unusually quiet.

To channel my energy into something useful, my older half-brother, Philip, who was 15 when I was then three, began teaching me the Arabic alphabet and how to count. In September 1939 at age three years and ten months my mother suggested to my father than I should be sent to first grade in school for me to learn and for her to have a rest from my mischievous behavior. At that time there was no minimum age for admission to school. My father, who was the school's vice principal, as well as a teacher, reluctantly agreed.

Father took me to school in September 1939 and introduced me to the teacher. She assigned me to sit in the first row of class. I was too short to reach the desk to sit normally so I climbed up on the seat and sat on my haunches. But to sit for fifty minutes without jumping around was impossible for me. Also, I knew most of the lessons being taught to the other kids. Whenever she asked a question I immediately answered it. The first time I replied she looked at me and said, "Before you answer you have to raise your hand like everybody else and wait for me to give you permission to talk.

Another time she said, "Keep quiet! You are disrupting the class. Wait for your turn."

I didn't like the teacher. I decided to spank her like my father did to me when I did something he disliked. Although I was too short to spank her butt, I jumped from my seat as she was writing on the blackboard with her back to us. I smacked her with my small hand on the back of her leg, just below her skirt. She immediately turned around and saw me. The other kids in the class were laughing. The teacher called the school secretary and told her that I was not ready for school. The secretary, who was employed by my father, agreed, took me to her office, gave me some candy, and called the custodian to take me home. Everybody on staff knew where my house was. He told my mother to keep me there until the following year. My mother was disappointed but I was happy to spend another year goofing off.

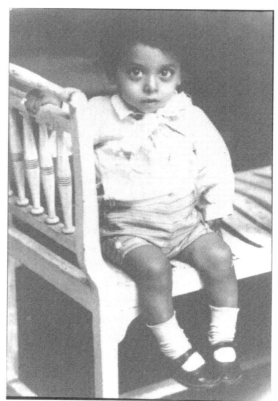

The author in 1938 at the age of three.

One event in particular is etched into my memory from my childhood years--the birth of my youngest brother, Rafik. I was seven years old at the time. As usual my father brought Om Ali, the midwife, to the house around 4 a.m. Rafik was born an hour later but there was a medical problem. My father sent for the obstetrician and the issue was resolved.

As was the custom, a few drops of sugar and water were put into the new baby's mouth, and he was wrapped in white clothing. I was intrigued to watch all this. Then my father went up to the rooftop and killed a chicken. He handed it to my aunt, who was visiting from Cairo, to cook. She made chicken soup and rice for my mother.

Even more fun for me that day was when my older half-sister, Hend, asked me if I wanted to go with her to the River Nile, a mile away.

"Of course!" I said.

The evening weather in late September was cool but not cold. Hend was carrying a package with her. When we reached the river she threw the package into the fast-running water.

"What's in the package?" I asked.

"That was the afterbirth," she replied. "It's an offering to the Nile to bring fertility to the land of Egypt."

On the seventh day of a baby's birth a celebration was held. Many neighbors and friends came by the house. First, they struck a brass handle on an object next to the baby. If it startled him it meant he had good hearing and good muscle response. I guess it was a primitive hearing test. Then came the big moment: the naming of the child. Three candles of equal length were bought from the store and lit. Each one was given a boy's name. The candle that lasted the longest decided the baby's name. My brother was thus named Rafik.

Chapter 2
OUR TOWN, OUR HOUSE

Beni Suef had 50,000 inhabitants. Government Square was the center of all the important buildings and included the civic center, the city hospital, the police and fire departments, and the Public Library. To the south of the square was the old city with its narrow, torturous unpaved maze of interconnected alleys, most of which had no numbers and were identified thusly: "Where do you live?"

"In the house next to the shoemaker."

To the north was the new part of town with wide main streets and side streets. Unlike the older part of town, the streets had names as well as numbers. Our house was on the corner of a main street and a side street lined with fifteen dwellings.

Detached Western-style houses were few and owned by the rich. Most people lived in apartment buildings of various sizes, two or three stories high, with one or two apartments on each level. Although our family wasn't wealthy, our house was special. It was bigger than the other houses on our street, with two floors and a huge flat rooftop. As with many homes on main thoroughfares, the street level frontage was designed for shops, and one of ours sold vegetables and the other sold falafel. At the back of the shops below our house was a large room that we used for storage. Our front door faced the side street and had a brass knocker. When visitors knocked we opened the door remotely from the second floor with an ingenious gadget. Tied to the second story railing was a rope that went down through a right-angle pulley

The Khalil family house in Beni Suef, as seen from the main street.

that was connected below to a latch. As we pulled on the rope from upstairs, it opened the door downstairs.

Our house had four bedrooms, a family room, a formal living room, and a dining room. All were spacious, with high ceilings. We entered our second floor through two doors off of the landing. The main door was in the middle; a side door opened to the living room. On one side of the house were the kitchen, bathing room, and a separate toilet, all connected by a long corridor.

The living room was filled with expensive, custom-made furniture. We were not allowed to play in that room as it was used mainly by my father for receiving colleagues doing business. The room was also where my father, a teacher, held his sessions tutoring high school boys in algebra every spring prior to the final examination in June. Thanks to its separate entrance, the students could come and go without bothering us. Each hour from 5 p.m. to 10 p.m. three boys arrived for lessons. My father earned good money from this extra job which helped to raise his nine children comfortably. When women visited women they did so in the family room, not the living room. As was the custom at that time, I never saw a husband and wife, except for relatives, visit us together as a couple.

We had no front or back yard. The houses were all built of limestone, which was abundant from the local quarry. Their stony walls stood touching one another as if for structural and moral support. Together the houses shared the sun and shade as the day progressed, and I fantasized as a young boy that they whispered to each other at night the secrets of their occupants. Walls have ears!

The best part for those who lived in houses like ours were the balconies, which were usually an extension of the family room or a bedroom. Constructed of wood, the balconies jutted out four feet over the street. Along the narrow side streets neighbors' balconies were a mere few feet apart. The balconies served as outdoor areas for many functions in people's daily lives. We had no air conditioning or heating but balconies facing north enjoyed cool summer breezes from the Mediterranean Sea, while balconies facing south enjoyed the warmth of the winter sun. Our family was blessed with a house that had balconies facing in both directions.

Men sat on their balcony early each morning drinking their first cup of tea and reading the newspaper. For children who were too young to play in the street, balconies were the perfect play area, and for women, the balcony was the main place for socializing with next-door neighbors and keeping up with the daily gossip and chit-chat.

With no telephones in residential neighborhoods, the news, good or bad, travelled from one balcony to the next at the speed of sound. During lazy summer evenings young men watched girls go by from their vantage point overhead. After a while, they became familiar with who was coming or going and with whom. Any change would spur surprise or speculation and demand further investigation.

Four of the rooms were bedrooms. The room I slept in had two queen-size beds. In one bed, I and my two younger brothers slept in a peculiar arrangement. We each had our own pillow. Two of us slept at the head of the bed, while the third boy slept at the other end in the middle. We got used to restless leg kicking by the three of us and slept soundly through the night. The other bed was reserved for my mother and the baby she was nursing, and one toddler.

The house in Beni Suef seen from a side street, showing a mosque across the street.

Another room had two beds for the four girls, my three sisters and half-sister, while a third room was for my two half-brothers. My father had a bedroom to himself, and my mother only joined him there when she was not nursing. He liked to have a good night's sleep with no interruptions from babies! These arrangements, of course, changed from year to year depending on the number of children at any given time. It also fluctuated when my half-siblings went off to college in Cairo during the school year and returned home to Beni Suef during the summer. Needless to say, no one ever had a room to himself or herself. As I reached high school my half-siblings were already employed in other cities. Thus, happily, the fourth bedroom was converted into a study with a desk, chairs, and a blackboard on the wall. I was a serious student and studied hard so I was grateful for the room's privacy.

Our beds were comfortable but mosquitoes and bed bugs were a problem to be reckoned with. Except for winter, mosquitoes were everywhere in town. Male mosquitoes needed only flowers to survive. Female mosquitoes needed a source of good protein from blood to produce their thousands of eggs. We kids were their source. To avoid being bitten, our beds had a mosquito net hung like a canopy from four tall metal rods, one at each corner. The nets were made from a very thin gauze-like fabric that prevented mosquitoes from getting inside but still allowed enough air to get through to breathe comfortably. Our nets were a sleep saver as we kept the windows open during hot summer nights. Amazingly, no one in our family got malaria, a common illness in Beni Suef from mosquito bites.

Bedbugs were rampant and they lived in the creases of the cotton-filled mattresses and in the metal springs of the open bed base. The only thing that killed bedbugs was kerosene. About once a month we would remove the mattresses from their base and spray kerosene all over the metal springs. As for the mattresses, we would pick the bedbugs from the creases with a piece of sticky dough. We usually got most of the adult creatures, but the eggs were hard to see and needed more periodic cleaning. We kept the windows open during the whole ordeal to dissipate the strong odor of the kerosene. Bedbugs don't transmit diseases but could disturb one's sleep, though over time we got used to them. There were always plenty of flies, too, throughout the day, and cockroaches at night. Over time I became an expert insect exterminator!

The family room and its large balcony facing the main street was the center of activity in our house. High on one wall there was a big shelf on which sat a large German radio. Only adults could reach the knobs on its lacquered wooden cabinet. For seating we had two makeshift sofas. Each was basically a large wooden box eight feet long, three feet deep, and two feet high. Inside the boxes my mother stored blankets, towels, and clothes not used for the season. A thin, soft cotton-filled cushion sat on top of the boxes with fluffy pillows at the back. There was no art on the walls, only family photos and a picture of the Virgin Mary holding Baby Jesus. We were Coptic Christians whose Greek church in Egypt was founded by the apostle Saint Mark. Our faith is close to Orthodox but diverges in some aspects.

The house in Beni Suef, as viewed from a neighbor's balcony showing structures on the rooftop.

On the opposite side to the living room were the kitchen, the toilet, the bathing room, and a narrow corridor connecting them all. The huge kitchen bustled with activity throughout the day. There was a wood butcher-block countertop, a sink, and a cabinet to store dishes, pots, pans, and utensils of all sizes and shapes. There were no gas lines and no hot water in the houses of Beni Suef. We cooked on four portable kerosene stoves that were fitted with a tank at the bottom. Three legs curved in at the top to hold cooking pots. In the center of each stove was a narrow valve with a very fine opening through

11

which the kerosene flowed upwards from a pressurized tank. Near the top of the tank was a screw cap for refilling the tank with kerosene. We used the stoves not only for cooking all of our meals but also for boiling water to take a bath or to wash clothes, or to make tea. At least one stove was on throughout the day. During meal preparation we could have three on.

Our kitchen window had a large ledge on which we kept a large box made of mesh screens. The wooden legs of the box were placed inside small cups filled with water. This way we could safely store food, especially desserts, overnight without having to worry about ants crawling in.

The toilet was small and constructed of a piece of marble on the floor with a hole in the middle. One had to squat above the hole to commence with the business at hand. The flushing tank was mounted high on the wall with a long pull-chain for flushing. There was no city sewer system. Every few houses were connected to a septic tank which was located under one side of the street and had to be serviced every few years. We had no toilet paper. Even if we did, it would probably block the narrow pipes with unsanitary and disgusting consequences. However, there was a water faucet, down low and reachable by hand and a large tin mug for cleaning. Our version of a French bidet. We learned to adapt. From age four we used that toilet. Before that age children used a tin pot, called a "kasria," which my mother would empty into the toilet. Our bathing room was separate, with a shower but no hot water. It was great on hot summer days but during the rest of the year we had to boil water in a five-gallon pot for bathing.

During World War II when Germany invaded Egypt our town was barely impacted except for a shortage of sugar and tea and a few other foods which were purchased using government-issued coupons based on the number of family members. I remember that soap was expensive and not readily available, so we used homemade soap. My father cooked a mixture of oil, potash and flour in a large pot for hours. It was then emptied into a rectangular metal container. As it cooled, it solidified. My father would cut it with a large knife into square pieces when it was just firm but before hardening. He made two kinds of soap: a general purpose soap with extra potash for heavy cleaning and a personal soap for bathing and washing our bodies. It had less potash, and a flower scent was added to it. Thus it was gentle and smelled good. After the war we bought soap from the store.

Our flat rooftop, accessed by climbing up a twenty-five-step staircase, was enormous. It was the same size as the whole house. The floor was made of limestone, and a six-foot brick wall surrounded the entire area. We had several coops for raising chickens, ducks, and rabbits, a large partitioned-off room with a country-style, wood-burning furnace, a storage room, and a sink with a water faucet. The rooftop was open to the sky. Toddlers spent most of their time playing safely there while the older kids played in the street. The house was truly our castle. No one lived above or below us. It faced the main street on a corner lot, had two balconies and a huge rooftop. Who could ask for more?

The streets were dusty and so were the houses. Most of the small streets were unpaved. On windy days, desert sand and dust filled the air. The paved main streets could get very hot during summer afternoons. A large city water truck passed through spraying water on the hot surfaces. In addition, shopkeepers sprinkled water on the sidewalks in front of their shops. Most stores closed in the early afternoon for two or three hours. Many men, including my father, took a siesta from 3 p.m. to 4 p.m. Children were expected to play in the street and give my father quiet time for him to sleep. Women didn't take siestas. There was always, it seemed, housework to do. These traditions were accepted as the Egyptian way of life.

There were a few parks at the edge of town with grass and trees but no flowers or a sprinkler system. The grass was well-cut with a manual lawnmower. The old caretaker, who lived in a shack at one corner of the park, watered everything with a long black hose. We enjoyed playing and running around in the open spaces. There wasn't any playground equipment, but there was a large gazebo in the middle of one of the parks where, on Friday evenings during the summer, the police department's brass orchestra performed. I was fascinated by the different shapes and sizes of the brass instruments that the ten musicians played. The park was always full of families sitting on the grass around the gazebo enjoying the free concert. Sometimes people brought sandwiches with them, but everyone had to drink from the park hose.

One of my favorite places was the city library. It was a wonderland to me. There were books for all ages that we could borrow for a week at no charge. No adult signatures were needed and the librarian trusted us. However, we would pay one penny every day a book was overdue. We learned to read fast and avoid the penalty! During the summers I read as many books, both fiction and nonfiction, as I could. There was also the Reader's Digest magazine available in Arabic. I especially enjoyed its stories about life in America and

13

how rich the people were, but I always wondered about the clever raccoon. The stories had him opening doors and I couldn't imagine what he looked like.

When I was growing up, Beni Suef had one fire truck. It was almost always parked in the fire station and was constantly being polished. I don't remember any fire ever breaking out. There were no police cars and our policemen patrolled on foot. Their priority was to keep people safe. At important intersections a policeman usually stood all night from 11 p.m. to 5 a.m. watching people walking into or coming out of their houses. Policemen knew the whole neighborhood they were assigned to. If they suspected any stranger walking in the area, they inquired into the purpose of his being out late and wandering around.

All in all, Beni Suef was an ideal place to live for families with children. Many small cities were safe and had most of the amenities we needed. Looking back, I realize how fortunate I was to spend my childhood and early teens there. Another advantage was that it was only two hours by train to Cairo, with its exciting new world of a university, museums, theaters, and the awesome pyramids of Giza.

Chapter 3
MY FAMILY

To me, my father was a hero and my mother was a saint. My success in life and that of my eight siblings is largely due to my parents' commitment and sacrifice.

My father's family was landowners in the countryside. Part of the land was fruit orchards where they grew mangos, oranges and dates. The larger portion, however, was for planting wheat, corn, and cotton. We always imagined that our grandfather must have been rich, as he built several apartment complexes in old Cairo at the end of the nineteenth century. After he and my grandmother died within a few days of each other in 1898 during an epidemic, each of his five children inherited one complex. My father, born in 1896, was the youngest of their children whose ages ranged from two to twenty-two. His oldest sister, who had been married with children his age, raised my orphaned father in Cairo. He must have been a good student as he was the first in his family to qualify for and receive a college education, becoming a teacher in 1919.

All of my father's siblings were married and lived in Cairo. They were decent but average folks. No servants and no speaking French like my mother's siblings. I even doubt that his three sisters went to school as I never saw them reading anything. His older brother died before I was born. My father married a distant cousin, Fariza, as was customary at the time, and had three children born in 1922, 1924 and 1926. His wife died during a fourth delivery in 1928 and so did the baby. My father was crushed. He asked a distant relative from the countryside, Om Wahba, an older widow, to come to

Beni Suef and take care of Philip (6), Boshra (2), and their sister Hend (4). Three years later, at the age of 35, my father wanted to marry again. He asked his older brother in Cairo, who was a government employee, to find him a wife through his connections.

My mother, Dawlat Ibrahim, and her family belonged to the aristocracy. They lived in Heliopolis, an upscale suburb of Cairo. Her father was a high ranking employee in the government with nine children. She was probably born between 1908 and 1910. Only boys needed a birth certificate back then as proof of age for the compulsory induction into the army at age nineteen, when Egypt was part of the Ottoman Empire. My mother and her siblings attended French schools run by nuns. They spoke French at home and played the piano. My Uncle Ramzy, mother's oldest brother, received a doctorate degree in law in Paris, and returned to Egypt with a French wife.

The Ibrahim family lived in a mansion with seven bedrooms. They employed a cook, a male servant, and a maid. They had a full time chauffeur for their private car. As a child, I enjoyed visiting my aunts and uncles especially when the chauffeur took me and a cousin of my age to an ice cream parlor a few miles away, waited for us, and returned us home. The most fascinating thing to me, however, was the buzzer hanging from the dining room chandelier. My aunts rang it for the servant to come running from the far-away kitchen. My aunts didn't cook. They didn't have to. During those visits, I enjoyed having a hot shower without having to boil water like in Beni Suef. However, I felt left out when they all conversed in French which I didn't understand.

My mother was very different from her sisters. She enjoyed cooking, and excelled at it. She was also humble and caring. My father was impressed with her. Her older brother, the lawyer, was in charge of the house as his father had passed away two years earlier. Uncle Ramzy admired my father's personality and entrepreneurial spirit.He agreed to my father's request to marry Dawlat, his sister. Girls at that time had no say in wedding agreements. However, shortly thereafter there was a clash between my uncle and my father because, as was customary, both families shared in the expenses of the furniture, jewelry and other furnishings for the newlyweds' house. My uncle wanted to buy her a piano.

"A piano? No, no. No one in Beni Suef owns a piano," said my father. "It's totally unnecessary."

Entertainment must have been the last thing on his mind with three young children, and more to come from a new wife. The piano was never purchased.

When my mother arrived in Beni Suef in 1931, she must have looked different from the town folks. She wore fancy dresses and a large hat with a colorful feather sticking out. I'm sure she must have looked out of place. Although her French was better than her Arabic, she made friends easily, and gradually fit in.

The author's father, Fawzi, in 1930.

Within a year of her marriage to my father she had a baby girl who died in infancy. Later she had another girl and then a child every two years thereafter for a total of six children. With my father's own children from his first wife, we were now a family of eleven. Babies were breastfed for a full year. My mother was either pregnant or nursing a baby for 13 consecutive years, from 1931 to 1944. She gave birth to Laila in 1933, myself in 1935, Ekbal in 1937, Nagi in 1939, Safinaz in 1941, and Rafik in 1943.

Men were not involved in any of the responsibilities at home. They were the breadwinners. My father's involvement was only to help us with homework. He was an easy-going man. Being a math teacher and a vice principal in the school he part-owned, he made sure that he never taught the first period of the day. This allowed him to sleep in and have a leisurely breakfast free of his children's commotion before leaving home. He returned around 3 p.m., ate lunch which was the main meal of the day, and then took a one-hour siesta. When he got up he checked our homework and helped us if we needed it. In the evening he went to an outdoor cafe in town to meet his friends, drink tea, play cards or backgammon, and listen to music. He usually returned home after we had gone to sleep.

My mother's life, in contrast, was hectic. We, like many middle class families, had a full time servant. Nonetheless, it was up to the lady of the house to organize and carry out all activities during the day.

Her daily routine rarely changed. She woke us early in the morning, prepared our breakfast, and helped the younger ones wash their faces, brush their teeth, and put on their school uniform. In addition to feeding the family, Mother shined our shoes every night, combed and braided the hair of my three sisters, and trimmed our nails once a week.

Mother made sure that we took our books and homework, and either made us sandwiches or gave us money for lunch. The worst part of the morning ritual was sharing one bathroom with my five siblings. We all had to hurry up to leave for school by 7:30 a.m.

After the children and husbands left their homes, many women neighbors visited with each other for a cup of Turkish coffee and gossip before starting the meal preparation tasks. There were no phones in the houses of Beni Suef, and our house was the hub for neighborhood women. We always had plenty of food and beverages to share. Women could also chat with their close neighbors across the balconies or through their windows. Some women preferred to visit in the evenings. They talked about food, their children, their husbands, but especially gossiped about other women in the neighborhood. Some stories were fascinating to a five year old. I often pretended to be asleep on the couch in the family room and listened to their stories before my mother would carry me off to bed.

Our oldest half-brother, Philip, obviously resented my mother and her children, often a typical reaction when two families are combined. When we were small and needing attention, he was a teenager who liked to boss us around. He argued endlessly with my mother. Frequently my parents, behind closed doors, had a shouting match which almost always included Philip's name. My mother often came out crying. Philip seemed to try and make the life of his half-siblings difficult, perhaps due to envy or bitterness. He gave us homework, even during the summer, from the time we were four years old.

The author's mother, Dawlat, in 1935.

My siblings resented him for making us study but could not object if they were to avoid a spanking. I, on the other hand, liked the homework, even before first grade which I entered at the age of almost five years old. I became Philip's favorite, as I was compliant with his orders. He even sided with me when my mother scolded me for something.

One summer at age seven, I came home crying after a fight in the street. He comforted me, but admonished my crying, saying "Big boys don't cry."

We used to eat a snack during the six hours between breakfast and lunch. A few days after the fight incident, I made the usual sandwich with feta cheese and pita bread. As I was eating, Philip walked into the room, snatched the sandwich from my hand and shouted at me.

"No eating between meals! It spoils the appetite and is not healthy!"

I was stunned. As he left the room I sobbed in silence. I was hungry and hurt, but I reminded myself, "Big boys didn't cry."

The three brothers on the house rooftop in 1951. From left to right, Nagi, the author, and Rafik.

The three sisters on the house rooftop in 1951. From left to right, Laila, Safinaz, and Ekbal.

Boshra, Philip's younger brother, and Hend, his younger sister, were nicer to us, but they generally kept to themselves. They had their own friends from the neighborhood. By the time I was in fourth grade, they had all gone off to college in Cairo.

My two younger brothers and my three sisters were usually nice to each other but when bickering with one another, my mother would say, "I'll tell your father to punish you."

He was the disciplinarian. My father was only five feet five inches tall but weighed more than 200 pounds. He had a strong and bellowing voice, yet deep down inside he was kind. When my mother told him about an incident he would decree, while sitting in his comfortable chair, that he would punish us severely. One whack with his heavy hand on our behind was enough to scare us. We learned, however, that his anger was shortlived. Whenever we heard his threat, we disappeared. If it was summer, we went out in the street. If it was winter, we hid under a bed. We stashed a pillow under my mother's bed to make our hiding time more comfortable. After he finished his cup of tea or coffee served to him by my mother, we would emerge, usually in less than half an hour. He then seemed either to have forgotten, or pretended to forget, that we were supposed to be punished.

Chapter 4
MY PRIMARY SCHOOL YEARS

In September 1940, at age four years and ten months I started first grade. Preparing for the first school day was a big thing. During the war, 1939 to 1945, there were no children's shoes sold in stores. Our shoes had to be custom-made. The shoemaker was an important person in our lives. He would come to our house in August with several sheets of white paper and a pencil. We'd line up for him to draw an outline of our bare feet on the paper and write our name on it. He would come back in a week or two for a fitting session. The shoes were always black, made of real leather, had long black shoelaces, and a strong leather sole. We were allowed one pair of shoes per school year, so the shoes had to last.

Very few families could afford to buy more shoes, even middle-class people like us. No doubt our feet grew during that nine month period, so the custom-made shoes were made a little too big at the beginning of the year. The fitting session included adding a thick insert so that we could walk comfortably. As the year progressed and the shoes got a little tight we'd put in a lighter insert made of cardboard or we'd take the insert out completely, depending on how much our feet had grown. The first few days in the new shoes were hard. The shoe leather was tough and sometimes caused a blister on the heel so we had to be very careful when we walked. A week or so later, the shoes became more comfortable as the leather became softer and sort of molded itself to the shape of our feet.

Shoes had to be shiny for school. Each day before class, the pupils lined up when the morning bell rang. when the morning bell rang. The school lieutenant, who was not a real army person but that was the name given to her, was responsible for discipline. We feared her. She was a big woman with a loud voice who'd walk along the line of pupils checking the cleanliness of the shoes and that the shoelaces were properly tied. Each Monday, which was the first day in the Coptic school week, we would also stretch our hands forward with palms facing down so she could inspect our fingernails to be sure they were short and clean. Every night, after my mother shined our shoes, she'd set them next to the door so we didn't have to go hunting for them in the early morning chaos. She would also cut our nails with a pair of large scissors on Sunday afternoons. Sometimes I was scared that she'd cut my finger, especially if I'd been misbehaving. Because I was always fidgety, she would say,

"Stand still, my love." She called each of her children "my love" with or without his or her proper first name.

School clothing was another issue. We all had to wear uniforms. The first three grades were mixed, boys and girls, and the uniform was the same and similar to the peasant's 'galabia', a one-piece dress made of cotton, off-white in color, with sleeves and pockets. From fourth grade on boys wore short pants and girls wore dresses. From fourth grade till the end of high school, boys and girls attended separate schools.

Our school bags, one for books and one for lunch, were made from similar cloth with two long ribbons threaded through the top so we could carry them on our shoulders. All these were hand-made by my mother who sewed everything for us, from home galabias, to school uniforms, to underwear, and undershirts. She spent many hours sewing for her large family's needs. Galabias were cooler in the summer and less restrictive of body movement. However, outside the home, western style clothes were the norm for us. The only items available in stores for kids were socks and leather sandals. Mending socks was another chore. When a sock was worn out, my mother would give it to us to add to other socks to make a soccer ball.

The first week in school was an exciting time. We were given the books we were to study that year but we had to buy our own pencils, erasers and notebooks to write in. We also had to buy color crayons for the art class at the beginning of the year and other materials as requested by the teacher for special projects throughout the year.

There were six periods during the day. We started at 8 a.m. with a fifty-minute period, and a five-minute break between periods which was for stretching and moving around. We were not allowed to leave the class except for urgent bathroom needs. After the second period we had a twenty-minute recess and after the fourth period we had one hour for lunch. During the lunch hour some kids went home while others stayed, ate their home-prepared lunch, and played in the school yard. There was no cafeteria or soft drinks. We only brought sandwiches and fruit from home. We had no drink containers, so we drank water from the faucet. There were no cups either, so we filled our little hands under the faucet and sucked the water up, using our pursed lips as straws. It would take several times to quench our thirst especially during hot days when we sweated a lot from running around. The afternoon consisted of two periods with no recess.

The distance from our house to the school was about 2,000 steps. Usually several kids from neighboring houses went and returned together to school for company. Some days, for one reason or another, I would return home alone. So I decided to count the steps. I liked numbers. However, it would be too much to count without distraction for such a long time. So I counted up to a particular corner on my way back from school and wrote the number down. The next time I would start from that corner to another corner and so on. As I reached home I added up all the numbers and it came close to 2,000. I don't know how big my strides were but it could not be more than one foot for a short six year-old.

One incident stands out in my memory. I heard cheering from the soccer field next to our school. I went over to watch. The players were very good. It was entertaining to follow the ball being kicked from one end of the field to the other and see the skill of some of the players maneuvering it to evade their opponents. I stayed for the whole game. My mother was concerned that I didn't get home at my regular time so she sent my older sister to look for me. There was obvious apprehension in the house when I walked in as they thought I might have been lost, hurt or kidnapped. When asked, I simply told them I didn't do anything wrong. I had no homework that day and the game was fun to watch. I got a scolding and was told never to do that again without permission.

During the winter of 1941, the school bought or rented a bus for the children as the weather was very cold. The bus would make the rounds to pick us up at designated street corners. We were ready long before it arrived in order to make sure we didn't miss it. The free ride only lasted a few weeks. One day the bus broke down in front of our house and it would not start. After a few attempts the bus driver gave up and said that he had to leave the bus overnight till he found a mechanic or spare parts in the morning. The buses had no automatic doors so the kids from the neighborhood played on it all evening. It was great fun. The next day the bus disappeared forever. I guess they couldn't fix it.

From that day on we had to walk to school all year round. It didn't rain that much but it could be cold and windy in January and very hot in May and June. Almost nobody had a car. I never saw a single kid in primary school come to school by car.

I loved school. It was fun to be number one, the best student in the class. Academics were my strength. However, I was not a talented artist and could not match my bigger classmates in sports. One reason for my success is that one of my older brothers, Philip, gave me the books for the following grade during the summer to study. I don't know if he really wanted to help me or if my parents told him to keep me busy and out of mischief.

Philip was strict so I worked hard to learn for two reasons. First, I loved books, and second, I was afraid to goof off as he would scold me. At the beginning of each school year, I would already know the subjects to be taught. During the first few days in second grade I irritated the teacher with my antics. I was not eager to sit quietly and listen as I already knew the material. She kept telling me to keep quiet so that the other kids could learn. It fell on deaf ears. One day she gave me a test which I passed easily. The following week they transferred me to third grade, skipping second grade. A year later they wanted to do the same at the beginning of the fourth grade, but I didn't do as well to skip that grade, too. Still, I was six years and ten months, a short and skinny kid in fourth grade. I remained at the top of my class despite being the youngest boy in the new all-boy school from fourth grade on.

During that school year, 1942 to 1943, there were a lot of student demonstrations and protests against one thing or another. High school boys would walk the streets by the hundreds chanting against the British as occupiers of Egypt, and French as occupiers of Algeria, though I wondered if some of them had any idea where Algeria was. Probably a few agitators knew what they were doing but the rest were glad to have a day off from school. In the middle of a demonstration some students would throw rocks at the glass windows of other schools, demanding that the boys of that school join their demonstration. In many cases, school administrators would let the kids out to

26

avoid school damage by those hooligans. I usually went home to study and play.

In the fourth grade we had to wear short pants, a short sleeve shirt and a fez, which was the traditional Ottoman Empire headdress for men and youth though we had not been under the Ottoman's rule for many years. I must have looked funny with that small red fez and dangling black silk tassel at its back. Early in fourth grade we had to rush out of the school during one of the demonstrations. My fez fell to the ground. Everybody was pushing everybody else to move on. I had no chance to bend down and retrieve my fez. It was probably trampled on by hundreds of boys. Better to trample a fez than to trample me, I thought. My fez was never found. For some reason wearing one became optional. I never wore one again. Unfortunately, I do not have a picture with a fez on my head to remember it by.

I loved math. After all, my father was a math teacher. In fourth grade we were taught the multiplication tables up to twelve. I decided arbitrarily that this was not enough. I figured out and memorized up to fifteen, as well as the square roots, and the second power to twenty. One day, a teacher sent a janitor to my class to take me to his seventh grade class. As I entered, the teacher asked me to solve some mathematical problems. I did. He then lifted me up in front of a thirteen year old boy and told me to slap the boy's face for his lack of mathematical knowledge. I refused. That boy was a known bully in school. I knew if I slapped his face and humiliated him in front of the class he would probably give me a good whack after school or even kill me. I was trembling as I went back to my class.

The teachers were knowledgeable but also tough disciplinarians. We were given homework every day and on weekends. If a boy misbehaved, he would be reprimanded. If the offense was serious he would be sent to the principal's office to be whacked. A custodian would hold the boy up. The principal would give the boy a few whacks on his behind with a six-foot bamboo stick. It must have been awful, but also humiliating. I never received any. Actually, I was to many teachers their favorite pupil. I don't know if it was my compliance, being the top student, or the son of a fellow teacher.

I remember a teacher who was responsible for tallying the whole year's test scores for the class. He gave me and an older boy the task of adding all the numbers of all the tests of all the boys in the class to find out the total score and ranking for the thirty-five boys. He gave us two days to do it. In those days there were no calculators so we had to do it all by hand. We finished it on time. He knew that I was accurate and would not cheat as I was the top-ranked student. I guess he was too lazy to do it himself, but it was fun and revealing to know the ranking of all our classmates.

The seventh grade final examination for primary school was a regional test, taken simultaneously by students from the Province of Beni Suef and another to the south. Our Coptic school produced the top-ranked student in the year before mine.

The author, age ten, in seventh grade.

In mid-year, the top three students were given awards in a large ceremony. I attended that event and our principal was one of the speakers. He praised the honored student as expected, but he also said at the end, "See you next year for a repeat."

He expected me to be the one. I was the youngest and smallest student in seventh grade at the age of ten. I was short and skinny, weighed fifty-five pounds and was only forty-eight inches tall.

Well, it didn't happen. The following June, I got top marks in Arabic, English, math, geography, history, social studies, and science. However, I barely passed the arts test. That placed me seventh highest of the 1,500 students who passed the test from the two provinces. Only two of the six who surpassed me were from our province and they were fourteen years old, three years older than me. One of them lived on a farm and soon joined the family business, while the other unfortunately died that summer from complications of typhoid fever. In high school I was the undisputed top student, and it was gratifying to see a plaque with my name on it outside the principal's office as the distinguished student of the year, at the Coptic school.

My father preferred that I leave the Coptic school after my primary school education, and attend the prestigious Prince Farouk High School in Beni Suef. At age ten years and ten months, I became a student at that school.

Chapter 5
THE GAMES CHILDREN PLAYED

Sports played a significant part in children's lives, especially as there were no television and no radio programs for children. We couldn't afford to buy any sports equipment, not even a ball. There were no community-organized sports in Beni Suef during my childhood and early teen years. Schools had teams but only the best students in any given sport would qualify to be chosen. Our summers were long, the houses had no air conditioning, and were always crowded with kids of all ages. Thus, we took to the streets for our sports and recreation. The streets were safe. I know that our parents were happy to see us get out of the house, especially my mother, so she could do the daily chores without interruption by the children. It would be quiet in the houses but noisy outdoors.

There were no adults involved in kids' sports on the streets. We handled everything ourselves, using whatever equipment or material for the games that we could make, find, or afford. The girls played hopscotch, jumping on one foot from one spot to another on lines they drew on the dusty street with a piece of stone. Another popular game, especially for girls, was skipping rope, with lots of variations like solo, double, forward, backward, fast, slow, and group jumping. It was an excellent exercise in agility and coordination. Boys sometimes played it too and occasionally we'd have a contest with our sisters. We won almost every time. I was good at it. It was tiring, however, to jump 100 times in succession, especially when it was really hot and we'd get too sweaty.

Knocking the Stones was a fun game. We would pile up flat pieces of limestone, found in every street, on top of each other with the largest one at the bottom and the smallest at the top. We could easily have a pile of ten pieces. Then we drew a line about fifteen feet away and stood on it to try to knock down the stones with a ball. Each person got five turns and the person who knocked down the most, won. It was a primitive form of bowling. The sizes of the stones varied depending on what we found on the street that day and the distance could vary depending on the age of the players. We'd be organized by age. A five year old would stand closer than a kid of eight or nine.

But the most important part of Knocking the Stones was the ball. No one but the richest families spent money for a ball of any kind. We improvised our own. We made them from worn-out socks and other material or scraps and leftovers from sewing. The ball's core was made of clumped-together pieces of old clothing, such as an undershirt. Then we'd fold socks tightly around it in succession, twisting them firmly till we got the right size which was usually six to eight inches in diameter. A good ball was firm and bouncy. Of course the color of the ball depended on the color of the outermost sock. We always used black or dark socks for the final piece so that the dust and dirt didn't show up as much. The last step was to sew up the top opening of the ball tightly. The more kids there were living in a house, the more worn-out socks there were and the better and bigger ball we could make. With my mother's help I proudly made the best balls on our street. We also played with marbles, and played hide-and-seek.

Another game we improvised was the backward throw of the ball. It was played by three to five of us. In that game, a boy positioned himself at a spot and three others fanned out behind him in different parts of the street, similar to first, second, and third base in American baseball. The boy in front threw the ball up and backward as far as he could. If one of the players behind him caught the ball before it hit the ground, he won. If the ball fell to the ground, the closest boy would run for it and try to touch the front pitcher with the ball before that boy reached a certain designated spot. Again, it was like baseball except we didn't use a bat and the ball was our homemade version.

The most popular game by far was soccer. It was played by almost all boys between the ages of five and fifteen. We had no need of a field. The street was our soccer field. We needed no posts for goals, either. We placed a pile of stones to mark the goalposts, usually ten to fifteen feet apart depending on the age of the players. The width of the field was the width of those narrow streets and the length was decided by how many players we had on each team, which could vary from three to seven. The center line was drawn by a stone in the dusty street. We played barefooted. With one pair of shoes a year for school, nobody dared wear them out in a game.

A soccer ball made of old socks.

Organizing soccer teams was a major issue. Almost every street had a team, and there was always an abundance of boys of all ages at any given time. The team usually consisted of ten to fifteen players. If there were too many boys, we would have two teams, one for the six- to ten-year olds, and the other for over ten years of age. Three members of the team comprised the board: a president, vice president, and secretary. They were selected by the team for various reasons. The president would be the oldest boy or the best player. The boy who had the best ball was assured a position. As we played for several hours at a time, the boy who brought water in a pitcher or better still, orange juice, was assured the other position.

There were a number of items for the board to take care of. The first was to give the team a name that usually signified its power. Our team's name was "The Ferocious Lion." The next street's team called themselves "The

Terrifying Tiger." Each team would paint on a house in that street the name of their team with water-soluble paint.

We played every weekend and every day during summer and other vacations. Even on school days, if we finished our homework, we'd go down and play with whoever showed up. Many kids had a ball for practice but the official ball for the team, and especially for tournaments, was the ball owned by a board member. We played among ourselves most of the time. However, there were tournaments with other teams in the neighborhood. Time and place were arranged by one of the board members with his counterpart on the other team. We were very organized and professional.

These neighborhood games were lively. The two teams shook hands before the game and an older boy acted as a referee. He wore a whistle on a string around his neck. He also had to have a watch to decide the length of the game which varied according to players' ages, how hot the weather was, and the number of players. Other boys who were not on the teams, as well as sisters of the players, would make up the spectators and each group cheered their team, clapping and shouting when they scored. The neighboring teams alternated the site of the games so that no one would have home advantage on his street.

The score of the game was written with chalk on the winner's street. No one would put his team's losing score on his street. So we knew if no score was posted on a wall of our street that we'd lost.

I always had a big jug of water for the boys to drink. My father's family owned an orchard about twenty miles away from our city. Every so often the farm workers brought us large quantities of oranges during the winter and dates during the summer. Since we had more than we could eat within our own family I often offered the boys oranges or dates during halftime. They were grateful. On top of that I had the best ball for a couple of years, assuring me Board membership.

At least half of the workforce in Egypt at that time was government employees who moved frequently upon promotion from town to town. So there were always new boys every year. One such boy was the son of a judge who was well-to-do. His father bought him a real soccer ball. We instantly elected him to the board. However, he turned out to be a terrible player but always wanted to be picked for the team. Most of the time that was acceptable. However, in one close game with a neighboring street team he was not chosen during the second half of the game and another boy substituted for him. He got angry, snatched up his ball, and ran off home. We had to decide either to keep him and the ball, or let him go, and play with our cheap home-made ball. We chose the latter as we didn't want to face the humiliation of defeat because of him. That was in the summer of 1944. The board then decided that we should have a real soccer ball so we all shared the cost from our pocket money savings. By Christmas we had a community soccer ball of which we were most proud.

One incident I'll never forget happened during the summer of 1943. Most of the time very few people passed through the side street where we played, usually only those who lived there. When someone walked by we stopped the game momentarily till he or she passed through our field. One time we were so involved in a hot match that we didn't notice the pregnant lady walking through. Unfortunately for us, the ball hit her bulging stomach. We thought we had killed the baby! We were horrified and we all ran off in different directions, disappearing in no time. We even left the ball in the street as the lady cursed us. Thankfully, there was no news of a birth, or a death of a newborn that day in our neighborhood, so it was with huge relief that we realized we must have done no harm.

There were no official coaches to teach us. Older boys taught those who were younger and took pride in doing so. We also loved watching regular school soccer games where we absorbed exactly how these trained children and youth played. Most kids stopped playing in the street when they got to high school age, except if they were asked to be a referee. We also followed the national soccer teams on the radio, and each of us had a favorite. Most of the pro teams were in Cairo and other large cities, but none in Beni Suef.

Another game, though much less popular, was volleyball. We couldn't afford a net so we tied a rope to a first-story balcony on each side of the street about six feet high, and drew the lines of the court in the dust on the street. But for this game our home-made ball was hard on the hands, and if a horse-driven carriage needed to pass through we would have to untie one side of the rope.

In 1946, when World War II was over, merchandise became more abundant and people had more money. So during that summer we decided to buy soccer uniforms. We bought twelve shirts of the same color. Each boy paid for his own. They were the pride of the neighborhood. But that was the last year I played in the street. During my high school years I had to study hard, and during the summers I joined the new Sunday School Club connected with St. Mary's Church

As for tennis, very few people played it. It was beyond the means of all but the richest kids. The only tennis courts in town were rented by the hour to maintain the clay and to pay for the custodian of the court. The rackets and balls could be rented too, but not the shoes. I never touched a real tennis racket in my childhood.

The same went for swimming. There was only one swimming pool and was part of the sports club with its exorbitant membership fee. Most children swam in the water canals and a few in the River Nile during its low season. My parents prohibited us from swimming in the canals or the river for safety reasons. There was a story about a teenager who climbed over the fence of the sports club after it closed at midnight one hot summer. He was found next morning at the bottom of the pool.

There was a store, no larger than twenty by twenty feet, resembling a large storage space. The owner had a lot of weights and advertised it as a weight-lifting club. One could pay a penny for a half hour of training. He coached the kids to assure safety and the proper use of weights. I tried a few times and was told by him that I had promising ability. I don't know if he was serious or just wanted to keep a customer. My father, however, discouraged me and said that carrying heavy weights at my young age while my bones were still growing would slow my growth and ultimately my height. Being short to begin with, I heeded his advice.

No one on our street owned a bicycle but they could be rented for two pennies an hour. Often two boys rented a bike together and shared the cost. In 1943, a boy fell off his bike and broke his arm. My mother then forbade us from riding and I never learned.

As I look back, I realize that a significant part of my personality was shaped by our street sports. Cooperation, compromise, managing anger, organization, teamwork, a good work ethic, the importance of training, and tasting both victory and defeat, have benefitted me throughout my life.

Chapter 6
THE KITCHEN HELPER

Feeding a large family in Egypt in the 1940s, when I was growing up, was an ordeal. There were no refrigerators in our homes. Very little food was imported and most ingredients for our meals had to be bought, cooked, and eaten the same day. It was a full-time job for women, in addition to feeding babies and cleaning house. Many families had a servant to help but from an early age chiren were given chores in the preparation of meals. I was my mother's kitchen helper during the summer, while my sisters were responsible for keeping the house clean.

Formal dining rooms were for guests only. There was no space in most houses for an additional dining table so many people, including us, used a movable table called a "tablia." Ours was a round, four foot wooden table on four short legs about one foot high. It was stored in a standing position in a corner of a hallway. At meal times, the tablia was rolled to the middle of the family room. Children sat cross-legged around it on the carpet. Rarely did my parents eat with us. We ate first. When we had finished a meal the table was wiped clean and rolled back to its corner until the next meal. Food was considered a privilege and not a right. We were taught to pray before meals. The prayer consisted of thanking God and our parents for providing the food, and asking God to feed the hungry.

Preparing the morning meal to feed six children at 7 a.m. began at 6:30 a.m. The favorite and cheapest food for breakfast was fava beans and falafel. The beans were prepared by cooking them slowly overnight in a large pot, and adding olive oil, lemon juice, salt and pepper. We scooped the beans from the dish with pieces of pita. The falafel was made from crushed beans mixed with green vegetables such as leek, green onion, spices and bread crumbs rolled into a dough. Small patties were shaped by hand and dropped into boiling oil for frying. Within two minutes they were ready to be scooped out, hot and brown and smelling delicious.

Falafel was usually eaten as a pita bread sandwich and topped with chunks of fresh tomato, cucumber, or tahini. The food was served on a single large dish placed in the middle of the table and we all dove into it. We didn't use plates and with six or seven of us at the breakfast table we learned to stretch out our arms and eat fast or go to school hungry! Breakfast was usually finished within ten minutes. We'd wash our hands in the one sink we had, get dressed, and leave for school at 7:30 a.m.

Certain stores specialized in selling falafel and fava beans and fortunately for us, such a store was on the street level of our house. My mother would shout from the balcony to Ali, the store owner. He would send one of his boy helpers to the curb under our balcony. My mother would tell him what she wanted and send down an empty container inside the woven straw basket. A few minutes later the order was ready for my mother to pull up. She would inspect it and when satisfied, she lowered the basket again with her payment.

We also drank milk, but buying it was another ordeal. There was no pasteurized milk in the stores. The milkman would make his rounds after we left for school. Fortunately, we were able to have milk at breakfast as we lived near the edge of town surrounded by farm land. One of my chores from age nine was to buy the milk in the evening from a farmer's wife. The cows were usually in the field during the day either grazing or being put to work, then returned to the farmer's house in the evening when his wife milked the animals as they arrived. There were barn-like rooms attached to the side of the house with large dirt floors where cows, goats, sheep, ducks and chickens slept.

My mother gave me milk money and a one-gallon metal can which I'd take to the farmer's house. His wife would fill it with fresh milk and I'd pay her. The hardest part of this chore was walking home at dusk for a quarter of a mile with a pot full of milk without spilling it. I learned to walk with steady hands, watching my feet on the uneven ground. I was lucky I never stumbled. As soon as I arrived home my mother would immediately boil the milk to kill any germs and keep it from spoiling until the next morning. She often made rice pudding with milk, sugar, and cinnamon for a snack before bedtime. Whatever milk was left over after breakfast was used to make yogurt.

Our big meal of the day was between 2:30 p.m. and 3 p.m. and was called lunch. The late evening meal was lighter and called supper. Early afternoon meals were timed for hungry children returning from school and hungry husbands returning from work. Preparing for lunch began shortly after breakfast.

Vegetable sellers paraded through town with whatever produce was in season. The most common were peas, beans, eggplant, spinach, cauliflower, cabbage, okra, tomatoes, and potatoes. A special vegetable during summer was called "molukia" which literally means "food of the kings." It had green leaves and made nutritious soup. Its preparation, however, was elaborate and time consuming.

Most often the sellers were men whose produce was loaded on a large wooden cart. The carts were about six feet in length and four feet wide, with two large wooden wheels, one on each side near the front. Close to the back were two wooden legs a few inches shorter than the wheel for the cart to rest on the ground when stopped. There were also two one-foot handles at the back of the cart with which to steer, and a ledge around the cart to keep the produce from falling out.

The sellers pushed their carts themselves. Few could afford a donkey. The carts were wheeled along slowly, with the seller shouting out how good his vegetables or fruits were in a melodic verse. Each seller had a distinct voice and made his own tune. They'd stop for a few minutes at the corners of the main streets to give housewives on the side streets time to hear them and to come down to buy. For the lucky ones who lived on main streets, women didn't have to leave the house. They bought whatever was needed using the dangling basket like we had.

I enjoyed hearing the songs about the produce. One such chanting, I remember some seventy years or so later, was by a grape seller. His tune, pleasing voice, and poetic lyrics were beautiful. It went like this:
> My grapes are the size of the eggs of turtle doves
> My delicious grapes everyone loves
> They are juicy and sweet
> At a price that can't be beat.

Women sellers had different ways of promoting their products. They had no carts but carried lighter loads in a large basket made of palm tree leaves.

They magically balanced the baskets on their heads without using their hands while walking along. Their main targets were the alleys and side streets. The women were often called to go up to the second or third floor apartments so that the lady of the house could inspect the vegetables before buying. It was easier to bargain with the female sellers, especially when they were tired after climbing up two floors.

There were also some grocery stores that specialized either in vegetables or fruit. They had a larger variety and carried heavy fruits such as watermelon. However, not all housewives could go to those stores. If they had a baby or a toddler that they wouldn't leave in the house alone, it was too difficult to carry a baby as well as her shopping. Thus, some shops, especially the fruit shops, were frequented more by men returning home from work. It was so exciting when my father brought home the first fruits of the season. Occasionally, at the height of the cantaloupe or watermelon season in the summer, a farmer would come to town pulling a donkey or, less frequently, a camel, with a large load dangling on each side of the animal's back in a big mesh net. We often bought several watermelons at a time and kept them in a cool place for a few days, usually under a bed, and ate one or two each day.

A farmer's market, held twice a week in a large square in town, was another way of buying fresh farm produce. The farmers, husband and wife, arrived early in the morning to unload the merchandise which in addition to fruits and vegetables might include chickens or ducks, wheat, corn, or dried beans. The wife sat at her designated spot to handle the selling while the husband went back to the farm to work. The marketplace was called a "souq." When I turned eleven, my mother entrusted me to go there with a basket and money to buy produce. My favorites were the delicious dates which came in red or yellow, and were soft or hard.

The buying process was an art and a source of amusement for me. Each seller tried to attract a buyer's attention by declaring that she had the most delicious produce at a reasonable price. Of course, no one but a fool would pay the asking price. People usually tasted the dates before buying. I went around tasting them until I was full. If I liked one kind, I would start the bargaining process. My first offer was usually so low it provoked the woman's anger. I pretended that her produce was not worth the asking price and started walking away, making her feel she was losing a customer. She lowered the price a little. I raised my offer a little. This game could go on for several minutes before an agreement was reached. The later it was in the day, the more bargaining power the buyer had, as no seller wanted to go back home with fresh but unsold produce, as the next market was three days away. Once we agreed on the price, the game of measurement began.

A street market in Beni Suef.

Most produce was sold by volume and not weight in five-gallon measuring containers. After filling a container I'd shake it vigorously to create space to fit in more produce. Finally, I'd give her the money and leave with my hard-won basket of produce. The whole process required training in patience, pretending to be angry, and retaining a sphinx-like expression on my face as I assessed the eagerness of the seller to settle on a price. This cat and mouse game was great fun and a battle of wits I greatly enjoyed.

Buying meat was a different issue. The government controlled the price and the days of operation. Butcher shops opened only three days a week except for the holy Muslim month of Ramadan when they opened daily. Cows, goats, or sheep were slaughtered very early on the designated days. Butcher shops opened from 9 a.m. until the meat was sold out, usually in the early afternoon. A few shops had a small freezer in case of unsold meat, which was rare. The carcasses hung on long hooks from the ceiling.

Different parts of the animal had different prices. Occasionally, the butcher cheated by giving a cheaper cut or putting heavy wrapping paper on the scale before he weighed the meat. One could not argue with a butcher wielding a big knife! We often gave him a little extra money than the government fixed price because this assured a good cut of meat. There were few butcher shops in town, so we made peace with the neighborhood butcher.

Chickens were another story. We raised our own on the rooftop at home. Each February we bought a hundred chicks during the hatching season. Throughout the year we ate the roosters and some of the hens, leaving the remaining hens to lay eggs. My father taught me how to kill a chicken by cutting a large vein in its neck. To avoid any spattered blood during the chicken's dance of death, I tucked the head under one of its wings. This method prohibited it from moving and the chicken bled in one spot until it died.

Preparing to cook the chicken was a job I excelled at. My mother would boil a large pot of water into which I dipped the chicken for thirty seconds. This made plucking the feathers much easier. I then cut off the neck and feet and opened the abdomen, removing its heart, kidney, and liver. The guts we gave to the cat. The chicken was then boiled with onions and spices. Afterwards it was cut into pieces and fried in butter to a golden brown.

We only ate duck on special occasions, fattening them up for three weeks before their demise. That was my job, force-feeding the birds with beans and corn. For that process I put my left leg above the back of the duck while sitting on the floor so it couldn't move. I held its head way up to keep the neck straight with my left hand and I opened the beak wide. With my right hand I shoved in a teaspoonful of corn or beans, and then stroked the food down through the neck. I did this daily. Within three weeks the duck would be so fat it could hardly walk. My mother often filled the cleaned abdominal cavity with stuffing made of unripe wheat, bread crumbs and spices. The meat was delicious.

My job in the kitchen was varied. We cooked rice almost every day. It wasn't sold in tidy clean packages but in fifty-pound sacks. It had a lot of impurities, other seeds, bits of straw, or even very small stones. The kitchen helper's job was to pick out all the unwanted stuff. For this chore one needed good eyesight, nimble fingers and endless patience. Another assignment was cutting large onions into small pieces to make sauce. I hated it, as it made my eyes water. Then came the tomatoes. There was no canned tomato sauce or paste. I had to squeeze several ripe tomatoes in a colander until all the juice filtered through, leaving the seeds and skin.

A kerosene stove from the 1950s.

The most elaborate kitchen job was making a soup from the nutritious molukia plant. First I had to cut the leaves from the long stem, wash and spread them on a large flat surface on the balcony to dry in the sun. We waited long enough for the leaves to lose some moisture but not too long in case they shriveled up. Then came the hardest part: mincing the leaves into fine pieces with a sharp metal dicer. After that my mother would take over, adding the leaves to the chicken soup along with fried mashed garlic and coriander. We would sip it with pieces of pita bread or mixed with rice. It was a favorite summer meal.

One of my mother's requests was that I would sing to her while she worked in the kitchen. I had a good voice, knew the lyrics of the new songs, and had a musical ear. The radio didn't broadcast continuously. There was no music when we were cooking from 10 a.m. to 1 p.m. To ensure a good performance I wrote down the lyrics to new songs and practiced the melody to perfection. With two or three noisy kerosene stoves in the hot kitchen, my singing added a joyous atmosphere!

Learning to buy and prepare food at a young age was an experience that lasted all my life, especially preparing me for my bachelor years both as a medical student in Cairo and through my early years in America. The memory of the kitchen sights, sounds and aromas in my childhood home remain vivid in my mind. Many of those dishes are still my favorites today.

Chapter 7
ANIMALS AND BIRDS

Animals and birds were everywhere in Beni Suef. They served many purposes in the daily life of every household. The most common animal was the donkey. In many towns and cities, including Cairo, donkeys were used to transport goods from one place to another. Farmers' donkeys pulled ten feet by five feet flat-top wooden carts filled with produce from their fields to sell. Women who came from rural areas to buy supplies they needed in the city shops would sit on the sides of the carts with their legs dangling on the way home, their purchases piled up in the middle.

Peasants without a cart used donkeys to carry produce in two large sacks, one on each side of the animal's body. A student in our high school came from a nearby village riding a donkey every morning. He would tie it up to a tree just outside the school fence. I felt sorry for the poor donkey because it had no food or drink throughout the entire school day. It was truly a beast of burden combined with stupidity. The worst insult was to say to someone,

"You're a donkey!"

The phrase was often used by teachers to students who appeared dumb and by parents to their kids if they misbehaved.

For us little boys, the most interesting part of the donkey was its penis, and what would happen when it urinated. For some reason, its hidden penis came out from its sac, became longer and longer, and reached, by our estimate, a foot of a solid rod! The urine poured out endlessly. After it stopped, the penis shrank and went back to its hiding place. I have never seen another animal with such a huge penis displayed so many times a day. We also heard that if a male donkey mated with a female horse, the offspring was called a mule, which in itself is genderless and could not reproduce. However, a mule had the strength of its mother, the mare, and the stupidity of its father, the donkey. This made it a better beast of burden than the donkey.

There were far fewer camels than donkeys. Camels were best suited for the desert because of their ability to go without water for days, and for their ability to tread carefully on the sand with their peculiar hoofs. As most Egyptian cities, towns, and villages were located on the narrow strip of non-desert land around the Nile, camels were unnecessary except for tourists traveling near the Pyramids. I never rode a camel while living in Egypt, only when I went back for a visit as a tourist. Camels, however, were abundant at the many oases scattered around the desert, both to the east and west of the River Nile, wherever there was enough ground water.

Camels were also used for certain jobs and occasions. For example, a farmer would use them to bring large, heavy watermelon loads to town as a camel could carry much more than a donkey. Another example was a bride-to-be parading through town sitting in a special cabin atop a camel, like Rachel and the other women did on their journey with Jacob in the Book of Genesis. The future bride would be followed by other camels carrying household items that her husband had bought for her, usually pots and pans, fabrics for making clothes, and small but fancy furniture, as if to show the town her nice new possessions.

Saudi Arabia was a poor desert country before the discovery of oil. Muslim countries, including wealthy Egypt, sent large quantities of cloth to Mecca to cover the Kaaba during the hajj season. Towns and cities contributed to that gift, parading on camels the offerings to be sent to Cairo, before reaching its final destination, Arabia.

A few rich people rode horses, but the main use for horses was to pull the carriages that were used for transportation. A few times a year an Arabian dancing horse show came to town. It was fun to watch those beautiful animals sway gently to the music, mainly provided by bagpipes. There was no horse racing track in Beni Suef.

Saudi Arabia was a poor desert country before the discovery of oil. Muslim countries, including wealthy Egypt, sent large quantities of cloth to Mecca to cover the Kaaba during the hajj season. Towns and cities contributed to that gift, parading on camels the offerings to be sent to Cairo, before reaching its final destination, Arabia.

A few rich people rode horses, but the main use for horses was to pull the carriages that were used for transportation. A few times a year an Arabian dancing horse show came to town. It was fun to watch those beautiful animals sway gently to the music, mainly provided by bagpipes. There was no horse racing track in Beni Suef.

A donkey-drawn cart in Beni Suef.

We had many other animals that were useful. Goats, whose milk was closer to human milk in composition than cow's milk, was easier for babies who had an intolerance to cow's milk. Sheep were highly valued, being raised for meat and wool. Their sheepskin was made into rugs and blankets and their wool into material that was woven to make cold weather clothing.

The most commonly used animals for meat and milk, though, were water buffalos and cows. Their hides were the primary leather for making shoes and luggage. As for milk, buffalo milk tasted richer, especially for making cheese. Peasants preferred it, for it produced more butter. But above all, oxen were the backbone of the farmer's workload. They were used for tilling the land, harvesting the crops, and moving water from the canals for irrigation or from deep wells. No machinery was used in the countryside while I was growing up.

The dung of all these animals was all over the streets, but it, too, had its uses. Peasant women routinely collected it in large containers to be sold later as fertilizer. If mixed with dry straw, these fuel cakes were excellent for heating home furnaces for baking.

Pigs were considered unclean by the Muslim majority. Egyptian Christians didn't eat them either. Pigs were raised by the Greek or Armenian communities. They were kept in enclosures during the day, but often let out at night to scrounge around the garbage bins on the streets that residents had set out for the garbage collector the following morning.

Dogs were detested by Muslims. In their tradition, if the shadow of a dog fell on them after they washed, as required before their daily prayers, they had to wash again. Thus, you could see men going to the mosque with a long stick in their hands, hitting dogs who came near them for no reason other than to avoid their shadows. They never hit sleeping dogs, however. Few people owned dogs in the cities but many did in the countryside, either to protect and guide their sheep, or to protect their property. In nearby villages, animals, which might include a cow, a donkey, sheep, goats, or dogs, slept in the inner barn that was called a manger. A thief had to go through the living room and bedrooms of the owner before they got to the manger. Thus, the animals were safe at night.

Cats were a different story. Most houses had them for practical reasons. Mice were everywhere. There was no cat food. A cat had to hustle for its meals. With many items stored throughout the year, from grain to cheese to dried fruits, mice could have a feast at all times. Even stray cats on the street were left alone to control the mice population. We had both a dog and a cat. They ate our food, but the cat always preferred the mice it caught. Sometimes it might be full, but it would still kill a mouse if it saw one, I guess out of instinct. It would then play with the dead mouse or kill it slowly. It was fun to watch for us boys. Girls were always scared of mice, whether dead or alive.

Rabbits were domesticated and raised at home for meat and fur. We had at least twenty at any given time. They were housed in a wooden hut on our flat rooftop. My dad was the only person in our family skilled enough to kill and skin a rabbit. Their meat was tasty if cooked the right way, and my mother was an expert. I never learned to catch a moving rabbit.

Other birds included domestic pigeons, which were a delicacy when roasted over a fire. They were, and still are, offered at fancy restaurants throughout Egypt. Swallows and some migrant birds flooded the area at certain times of the year. They were caught, sold, and cooked the same way but were not as tasty as home-raised pigeons.

I heard of people observing foxes and an occasional wolf at the edge of town. However, I never saw any myself, or heard of an incident related to them.

Birds of prey, though, were familiar sights in Beni Suef. There was a family of hawks that made their nest on top of a mosque's minaret near our house. I was told that hawks fed mostly on field rats, of which there were plenty. The hawks occasionally snatched chicks from neighbors' roof tops. We kept our chicks unattended indoors, but I guarded them with a stick in my hand if they were out of the coop. We never lost a single chick. Adult hens were not in danger.

Ravens periodically appeared in large numbers from nowhere. They mostly snatched scraps of meat or dead animals on the streets before cats or dogs could get to them. A dreaded bird was the owl. In Egyptian culture it was a bad omen to see an owl on one's house. It meant either an imminent death or a calamity in that house but I don't remember any such things happening. Owls were good nocturnal hunters of mice and rats, sharing the task of clearing out these critters with the cats.

During a visit to Beni Suef ten years ago, I didn't see any more hawks. Their nest was gone. I didn't hear any owls, either. I was told they were extinct, probably due to environmental reasons. I don't think that it was due to a lack of food, as the mice and rats were as abundant as ever in Beni Suef.

Chapter 8
THE CHICKEN AND I

Domestic hens are the only birds which lay many more eggs than they can possibly brood. Thus, they provide us with an excellent source of protein and iron day after day.

During my childhood in the 1940s in Beni Suef, as in all small cities, towns and villages in Egypt, most people raised their own chickens for eggs and meat. For the few houses with a backyard, the chickens could roam inside and often outside the yard but always stayed nearby.

People built rooms or wooden huts on their rooftops for various purposes. We had a large hut as a chicken coop, another for rabbits, a third for other activities, and a large room with an enormous oven for baking. The middle of the roof floor was wide open for chickens, ducks, geese, turkeys or whatever we were raising at the time. They would move around by day but get inside the rooms or huts to sleep at sunset.

My family kept at least twenty egg-laying hens throughout the year. When I was twelve years old, I was put in charge of the chickens for three years. I enjoyed my job immensely and it gave me unparalleled life experiences.

The day started with the rooster announcing to his harem, the hens, that it was time to get up. As one rooster crowed, other roosters from various houses responded. It became like a symphony with roosters as the musicians. After a while I was able to distinguish the sound of each rooster and its distinctive melody. At daybreak I would go up to the hen house to let them out to eat, exercise and lay their eggs. I spread a measured amount of corn for them, and filled a large bowl with water before going to school. I did the same when I came home during the school year. My mother was responsible for them in the daytime. However, during summer and winter vacations I was totally in charge of the chickens.

There was a certain pecking order in which they ate. Once they saw the food the rooster stood guard, letting his favorite hens eat first, then other hens, and lastly himself. A good rooster is truly like the responsible captain of a ship. Their evening meal was different from the morning corn. I often mixed bran with left-over food. It might be soup, or a vegetable casserole, which they loved. I also noticed that chickens liked to eat the dirt wedged into the soles of our shoes.

Chickens roaming the countryside ate the feces of animals and humans, which was strange and unsanitary to me. However, I learned that, through instinct, the chickens knew what their bodies needed. The soil and clay in our area was rich in lime and from this the chickens got calcium to form a good shell for their eggs. Humans also get iron from food but because our bodies only absorb ten percent of the iron, the rest passes out through our stools. Iron is necessary to form good egg yolks, essential if the egg is to hatch a healthy chick. Thus, chickens managed to find the food they needed.

Our method of providing a safe and private place for the chickens to lay their eggs was simple. We half-filled two glazed clay containers with straw. They were two feet in diameter and two feet deep and called "magoors." They were placed in a corner of the rooftop. The hens liked to jump into the magoor to lay their eggs. I often watched from a distance as the egg protruded slowly from the behind of the hen, and finally fell gently onto the straw bed. Once done, the hen jumped out, leaving the birthplace for another hen. This process of labor usually took ten to fifteen minutes.

Sometimes more than two hens were ready to lay their eggs at the same time. They made distinctive sounds which became louder with the urgency of the situation, as if begging the hen occupying the magoor to hurry up. I also noticed that hens had a favorite magoor, using one of the two containers consistently to lay their eggs. They would use the other container when their regular container was continuously occupied. They often stood next to their container, as if in a queue, ready to hop in as soon as the egg-laying hen got out, thus beating other hens waiting to deliver.

One summer, I noticed that the eggs were not exactly all the same shape. I collected the eggs immediately after each hen laid hers and to my amazement

I discovered that each hen laid the same individually-shaped egg day after day. Thus, at the end of the day I could tell which hens laid and which didn't, that day. One hen always laid very oblong eggs. I found that they had two yolks. I wondered whether, if these eggs were to be hatched, twin chicks would result. I never got the answer, but I learned that the anatomy of the hen's reproductive system dictated the shape of the egg. The hen with the double-yolk eggs probably had a semi-divided womb.

Hens laid about thirty to forty eggs during a two-month cycle, then stopped for a month before the cycle began again. When we killed such a chicken for food we found grape-like yolks of various sizes, representing the level of growth for each upcoming egg. I calculated that it took about two weeks from the beginning of growth of a pea-sized yolk to a mature egg with a shell. It was astonishing to discover that it took only two or three days to form a strong shell.

I noticed one hen going well over a month without laying eggs. She was not too old to stop laying. I told my mother about her. That hen was our next day's meal. I found a large tumor in the uterus (like a fibroid) preventing the tiny eggs from having space to grow. We were studying biology in school at that time. Those observations made me more eager than ever to learn about all living things.

The sex life of a chicken was very interesting to a thirteen-year old boy. I noticed that the rooster mates with the hens frequently but mostly at the beginning and end of the day. This way the rooster's semen assures that it sticks to a yolk at the right time before the protein of the egg white forms around it. Thus the eggs were always fertile and assured the survival of the species.

Hatcheries usually produced the largest crop in February each year and chicks were sold all over town. We usually bought a hundred or more of these noisy but beautiful chicks with fuzzy short yellow hair. They grew fast and during their second month small feathers developed on their little wings and the rest of the body. At about this age one could start differentiating the cockerels from the pullets as little red combs grew on the heads of cockerels. We immediately separated each gender, otherwise the adolescent cockerels would vehemently fight one another for dominance over the young females. We guarded the chicks in many ways, protecting them from the hawks that would snatch them from above, or the cats and the weasels from below. We

51

usually ate the roosters and left as many young hens as needed for their eggs.

It was so much fun to hear the first crow of the young cockerels with their thin, small high-pitched voices. During the following few weeks, their crowing became thicker and louder. There was one event I'll never forget. One day as I was feeding the pullets I found one of them mounting another. I was puzzled. I knew from observation that male dogs occasionally mounted each other when there were no available females during the mating season. But I never thought of a lesbian hen. How strange and intriguing! I didn't tell anyone as talking about sex, even among animals, was not polite. A few days later I heard a little crowing sound coming from the pullets' area. I entered and behold! That little bird was developing a little comb. Mystery solved! It was a late blooming cockerel.

Our hens laid ten to fifteen eggs a day which I collected and gave to my mother. They were used for a meal or for baking. A month before Easter my mother would remind me that I needed to collect a hundred eggs for the celebration. I'd hide some every day. We had no refrigerator back then but I found a secret place. No one ever discovered where I hid the eggs. When the big baking day arrived shortly before Easter, I'd give my mother fifty eggs. The other fifty I kept when the day came for us to color them.

Occasionally a hen would long for motherhood and she'd sit on the eggs as if trying to hatch them. I could always tell which hen was ready for the task from the sound they made shortly after they stopped the egg-laying cycle. With my mother's approval I would take one of the stoneware pots, place twenty eggs over straw in a store room that was seldom used, and let the broody hen sit on them. Those hens took their job seriously, only leaving the eggs for a few minutes to eat, drink, and move around the room before getting back to their eggs. If anyone came in while she was eating, she would jump back into the pot as if to protect the eggs from an intruder.

Chicken eggs hatch after twenty-one days, give or take one day. It was so much fun to walk in the room to put food and water for the hen in the morning and find that two or three chicks had hatched during the night. I would take them immediately to the chick nursery which was a large cage made of bamboo. The hen didn't mind me taking the babies to be fed. Eggs that didn't hatch after twenty-three days were usually either not fertilized, or somehow the developing chick died early, in which case we'd find a small glob of red tissue inside the yolk, a kind of miscarriage.

One time I broke one of those eggs that failed to hatch after twenty-three days and found a tiny chick. I thought it was dead, but was thrilled to see it breathing. I took it to my mother. She instructed me to wrap it in cotton and keep it warm in a cloth drawer. I did. To my surprise, the next day it could stand on its feet but was unable to feed. I kept it another day. It looked smaller than the other chicks but when it joined them, the chick began eating. I guess it was a premature chick and the cotton and warmth acted like a baby incubator.

One day in the egg laying period of a duck, I wanted to experiment with cross fertilization. I knew that mating a donkey and a horse would lead to a baby mule but I didn't know what the outcome would be from a male turkey and a female duck. So I put the turkey on top of an egg-laying duck. To my amazement he made mating movements. I waited thirty-five days for the eggs to hatch. Alas, all were regular duck chicks. I didn't know about genes or chromosomes, but it certainly made me more interested in biology.

We also raised ducks and geese. It takes thirty-five days for baby ducks to hatch and those chicks were the most beautiful of all the birds I had seen. I would take them the day they hatched and place them gently into in a large, three-foot diameter container filled with eight inches of water. The ducklings would immediately swim, a beautiful sight.

I learned a great deal about life, biology, and birds' social interactions, which gave me a deeper understanding of nature and some of its creatures.

Chapter 9
REPAIRMEN AND SHOPKEEPERS

Many of the household items we owned had to last a lifetime. Furniture often needed upholstery, appliances needed repair, and other items needed maintenance. Repairmen were essential in the life of everyone.

We cooked over kerosene stoves. There were no electrical appliances and no gas lines in the homes. Each area of the city had its own kerosene stove repairman. Ours was named "Taha." He passed by daily, stopping briefly at each street corner and shouting with a loud but pleasant voice over and over, "Taha repairs your kerosene stove!"

Women heard him through the open windows and called him if needed that day. He stayed a minute or two at each corner. If not called upon, he moved on. Hardly a month passed without us calling Taha at least once. My mother usually waited until two stoves out of our four needed repair before calling him. He would ascend the twenty steps to our second floor and sit on the landing area just outside the door to do his repairs. We liked to sit near him while he was working. He was a good story teller. Some of his stories were incredible but we believed him. When a kerosene stove he was fixing suddenly lit up, it seemed to us as if Taha had brought it back from the dead. He usually stayed about half an hour. My mother always made tea for him and if it was lunch time she would make him a sandwich.

Another important man in our domestic lives was the copper polisher. All the cooking pots were made of copper. With time, the pots would lose their luster and if left for long, acquired a patina discoloration which was thought to be bad for our health. About once a year, my father would arrange with the copper polisher to come to the house and polish all the pots and pans. The man did his work in front of the street gate of our house. He used chemicals and high heat torches. I guess the fumes emanating from the chemicals were dangerous as he wore a mask while working. When finished, the pots would be as shiny as silver. It was a whole day affair which meant that there would be no cooking that day. We would eat sandwiches of cheese or cold cuts. We were not allowed to get near him but we watched from the balcony. It was hard work. He had to rub the chemicals on the inside and outside of each pot and then direct the flame to every part of it. When cool, he wiped it vigorously followed by washing and then wiping it again with a soft cloth.

Another man who came to the house every two or three years was the upholstery man. He primarily worked on mattresses and pillows. These were filled with fluffed cotton which over time would sag and be uncomfortable to sleep on. He did all his work in one room of our house with the windows wide open. He'd open up all the mattresses and pillows and remove the cotton, which almost filled the room. Then he started beating on the cotton with what looked to me like a large metal rod. The cotton fibers filled the air. We could watch through the half-open door of that room but were not allowed in. Actually, it was boring to watch. At the end of the day, he put back the fluffed cotton in the pillows and mattresses. They were no longer lumpy and became very comfortable. I never saw him wearing a mask. I wonder now how his lungs ended up after years of inhaling cotton fibers.

There were a multitude of other men who performed specialized jobs in their stores instead of coming to the house. One of the most interesting jobs was the coffee bean grinder man. There was no instant or ground coffee, and no machine to do it at home. He used an ingenious way to do the job. In the middle of the store there was a large coffee grinding machine. The energy was supplied by a blindfolded donkey hitched to it and walked in circles around it. Sometimes the donkey got tired or perhaps bored of these endless circles. The owner would offer him alfalfa to keep him going. Sometimes he hit the donkey with a stick or would simply prod him with a special command in a loud voice. Fortunately for the donkey, there was not enough work for him to fill the day. In 1948 the store acquired an electric grinder. I never saw the donkey again.

When there was little going on in the shops, the owners from adjacent shops would sit together on a bench and drink tea. If one of them could read, he read the daily paper aloud to the others. If none of them could read, they usually asked a passerby whom they knew to come and sit with them, drink free tea, and read the paper. There were often heated discussions about political stories that usually ended amicably by one of them declaring, "The hell with all the politicians! No matter what parties they belong to, they are all crooks!"

Everyone agreed and they'd change the subject. When a customer came to any of the adjacent stores, the discussion ended.

The barber shops were for men only. Boys beginning at age three got their hair cut about once a month. No long hair was allowed for boys or young men. It was fascinating for me to sit on a child's booster chair and watch in the mirror in front of me as the barber used his scissors skillfully to trim my hair, walking around me. It was scary, however, to see him shave men's facial hair. He used a long sharp blade that looked like a knife which was sharpened by striking it on a piece of leather over and over. The best part was when the barber sprinkled scented water with a touch of cologne on my hair before combing it. It smelled so good, but didn't last long.

For some reason, the barber shop was often the meeting place for young men, especially during summer vacations. They all sat on a bench outside the shop in the fresh air talking and joking. The barber often participated in the discussion with them as the door was usually open. Sports and sex were the favorite topics, and occasionally, their family life, politics, and the movies. There was never a dull moment. It was entertaining.

There were very few such shops for women. They called them beauty salons. Women usually cut or braided the hair of their daughters or themselves at home. They only went to the salons if they were going to a party or a wedding. The front of the salon was not all glass as in the barber shops, where passersby could see who was getting a haircut. The ladies shop had a thick curtain, I guess for privacy.

There was no such thing as a supermarket. Instead, there were many small shops with narrow specialties. The butcher shop sold only meat, mainly beef and lamb. Fish was sold in the morning in an area next to the River Nile. Whatever they caught the previous night and early morning was displayed on a wooden cart. Usually their catch was sold out by 10 a.m. It was fun to watch the live fish wiggle in the seller's hand. Vegetables and fruits were sold mostly by wandering salespeople, but there were a few stores as well.

There were stores that specialized in nuts such as freshly roasted peanuts and walnuts which were used a great deal in making cakes, and all sorts of seeds like sunflower seeds, watermelon seeds, and many others. These were cheap and bought by people of all ages, especially teenagers who liked to snack on them walking by the river during the lazy days of summer.

A shop selling baskets woven with palm tree leaves. These baskets were used by sellers of fruits, vegetables, and grains.

The most important store, however, was the corner store owned by Kamal. Like 7-Eleven stores today, it carried cheeses, cold cuts, and pickled everything, from cucumbers to carrots to olives. It had a large refrigerator where we bought cold Coca-Cola and other soft drinks in the hot summer. I will never forget how helpful Kamal was. He lived near the store. In 1944, penicillin, the new wonder drug, was out on the market. It had to be given by injection in the muscles every three hours, day and night. It also had to be refrigerated until used. One time an old lady in the neighborhood had pneumonia but like everyone, she had no refrigerator in which to store the penicillin. Kamal volunteered to put it into his store's refrigerator. His store was only open from 6 a.m. to midnight but he would wake up at 3 a.m., come to the store and deliver the penicillin bottle to the lady to be given by a neighborhood barber who knew how to give shots. He did this for several nights. The woman survived her pneumonia. Kamal's kindness saved her life.

The tailor made our suits and short pants. The preferred material was English wool. It was expensive so nothing went to waste. Hand-me-downs were the norm. As children grew fast, it would have been unreasonable to make a suit every year for every boy. Frequently, the tailor would use my father's old suits to make our suits and pants from the fabric. He just turned it inside out and it looked like new. We wore short pants and a white shirt during spring and fall, and a knitted sweater in winter. Girls' clothes were made at home by their mothers.

The drug store was a very important place. Pharmacists were called doctors and acted as such. No prescription was required for many drugs treating common ailments, including the few antibiotics available in the 1940s. A patient would describe the symptoms to the pharmacist and be given the appropriate medication. It was successful ninety percent of the time. This way we avoided paying doctors' fees and long waits in their offices. There was another store selling natural cures, herbs and the like. Many of the plants, seeds and powders had strange names and some came from China. Many women bought powders for their skin and potions for rejuvenation, while men bought aphrodisiacs.

Chapter 10
WOMEN HELPERS

Life in Beni Suef was hectic for wives with many children. There were no birth control pills and no commercial milk formula for babies. Hence, many wives between the age of eighteen and forty-five were either pregnant or breast feeding a baby. Babies were weaned at one year of age. Shortly thereafter wives got pregnant again. Miscarriages and the early death of babies took its toll. Of fifteen or twenty pregnancies, only a few would survive.

Husbands took no part in house chores, especially the kitchen which was out of bounds for them. The most they would do was to help their children with homework. Women, pregnant or not, breast feeding or not, were totally responsible for taking care of the family and all their needs. Cooking for and feeding a family was a full time job by itself, from buying fresh vegetables each morning to washing the dishes at night. In addition there was laundry, mending socks, and giving us a weekly bath, which was a half-day job for six children. This left no time for other important family needs.

Many women were needed to help my mother, some for specific jobs, and one was a full-time live-in servant. The first servant I remember was named Aziza.

When Aziza came to work for us from a nearby village she was eleven years old. She stayed with us for a few years. There was the usual agreement between her father and my father that was similar for all servants. The girl lived with our family with full board. She received a stipend once a month but didn't personally take the money. My father would deposit it in a bank, or keep it under the mattress. It was saved until the time came for her marriage which was usually at the age of fourteen. Servant girls got noticed by village boys during summer. These servant girls were more likely to find a husband early, as young men knew that they would make good housewives, having been trained in the city by well-to-do families. The saved money would go to pay for wedding expenses.

Looking back, I feel sorry for Aziza, but that was the norm. She would wake up before we did to help with the preparation for the children's breakfast and go to bed after she had washed the dishes at night. She ate the same food as we did, but ate alone in the kitchen after we finished. She slept in a corner of a hallway with a thick blanket under her and another over her. She folded both in the morning and kept them in a closet. My mother sewed her clothes as she did for us, but Aziza wore no shoes, only slippers. Shoes were custom-made and expensive. Peasants wore no shoes in the country.

From morning until mid-afternoon during the school year, she helped my mother in meal preparation. Later in the day she washed the dishes. She was not involved in bread baking or clothes washing as those chores were done by women specialized in those jobs. Occasionally, Aziza would go with us to the nearby park in late afternoon. She was only a few years older than us, but was in charge of our safety. There was no distinction between her and us when we were playing. We were all children. Sometimes, other children with their servants were also in the park. Occasionally Aziza and the other servants congregated, swapping stories but at the same time watching us.

One of the worst memories I have about Aziza was when she got circumcised at age twelve. Girl's circumcision was a well-established custom in the countryside. The reason was that through circumcision, a woman would not enjoy sex and therefore she would not seek sexual gratification outside of marriage if her husband for some reason withheld sex from her. Thus she would not cheat on him. Sexual enjoyment was for men. Labor pains were for women.

Circumcision of both boys and girls was done at home by a town barber for boys and a midwife for girls. Boys were circumcised as infants in both Muslim and Christian traditions. Girls were only circumcised if their family wanted it and could be done at any age before marriage. I was seven years old, playing soccer in the side street when I heard screams coming from our house. It was Aziza's voice. I knew that my father never hit Aziza but I'd seen an unfamiliar woman entering our house a few minutes earlier. I didn't know what she was doing to Aziza. I only knew that girls didn't have what boys did, but I dared not ask that question. I didn't know if they used any numbing medicine on Aziza, but even if they did, it was obviously not enough. I wanted to sneak in the house under the pretense of needing a drink of water. The door was locked. Shortly thereafter the woman left. For a couple of days Aziza did no house chores. She walked for a few days with a clumsy gait with her legs slightly apart. It must have been awful for Aziza, but it must have been by her father's orders and any future prospective groom's desire.

Christian families had Christian servants, Muslim families had Muslim servants. Families often talked about religious issues at home, so it would have been awkward to have a person of a different religion around. During religious holidays such as Christmas and Easter, Aziza went to her village to spend a few days with her family. She also went home during the summer to help in the fields.

Aziza couldn't read, write, or do simple math, so my mother always checked after Aziza came home from the market to see if she was given the right change. She was happy to live with us because at her home she slept on a dirt floor, like everyone else in her family. We also heard, periodically, servants in the neighborhood being beaten by their masters. It was common for children, including servants, to be beaten for the smallest mistake. Child abuse was not in our vocabulary. The police were never involved. My parents never hit Aziza, but maybe scolded her if she repeated the same mistake, as they did with us children too.

When Aziza was fourteen, her father came to take her away and asked for all her belongings and her money. She was going to be married. A year later we heard that she had a baby boy. After Aziza was gone, we had several girl servants in succession. They were all from poor families in town, not the countryside. None of them were satisfactory. They were older, fifteen or sixteen years of age, and were not live-ins. They went to their homes at night. The first servant was lazy and goofed off a lot. She'd go shopping and stay much longer than necessary. She was not very helpful around the house either.

"I would rather do the job myself than keep after her to do it," my mother said, and let her go.

The second one was dishonest. She would tell my mother that the price of whatever she bought was much higher than it really was. Once my mother was suspicious of the amount of tomatoes the servant bought. We had a balance scale at home and discovered that the girl had bought three and half pounds instead of four. Also, a few small things went missing. My mother let her go.

The third servant was a good-looking sixteen year old girl. She worked well and was very helpful to my mother. However, we heard that she sneaked out at night to be with boys and men. Suddenly she disappeared for a few days. My father heard that she went to another town to have an abortion. Whether the news was true or false, he decided to let her go. After all, there were teenage boys in the house. She could claim one day that one of us made her pregnant, which would have been a disaster as there was no way to disprove something like that. There were no known paternity tests at the time. She was the last servant we had. My mother, for some reason, stopped having babies and we were able to look after our own personal needs. We no longer needed servants.

Preparing food and meals daily took half the day. With many other responsibilities, my mother needed help from several women; most notable were the washerwoman, the baker, and the cheese maker. These were hired by the day and each served several households in the neighborhoods.

In the 1940s there were no washing machines or hot water in Beni Suef. Our weekly wash day was Saturday. The washer lady arrived about 8 a.m. and finished about noon. She was in her fifties, heavy-set, dressed in black, and had a soft voice. A ten-gallon copper pot on a large kerosene stove was continuously filled with water and kept boiling, which the woman used as much as needed. The clothes were divided between white and color. Each was washed separately. They received five cycles: soaking, washing with soap twice, and rinsing twice. The soap was home-made with a much higher potash than the soap for bathing. The woman sat on the floor, spreading her legs around the large aluminum container which was about three and half feet in diameter and one foot high. She scrubbed every piece of cloth between her two hands. I felt sorry for her as her skin was badly wrinkled and unusually white from all that potash and hot water. What a way to make a living. She did this every day in different houses.

After she finished the rinsing, she put some blueing liquid with the white clothes which gave it a brighter white. Then she hung the laundry with clothes pins on several ropes strung between opposite ends of the roof top. My mother usually gave her lunch and money. Either my mother or some of the kids would go up and take the clothes down before sunset. In Egypt they were always dry by then, unless it was a rainy day which happened only a few days a year.

Baking days were fun. We baked large Arabic pita bread and many kinds of biscuits especially for special occasions such as Christmas and Easter. The baker, a woman, came around 4 a.m. My mother would have prepared the amount of flour for her and the yeast needed. The kneading was all done by hand. It was not unusual to bake fifty pounds of flour at a time. It took all morning to get the dough well fermented and ready for the oven. The furnace was built in a special room on our roof. It had a fireplace on the bottom, and over it was a glazed heavy flat surface. We used three kinds of material for fuel: dried corn stems which burned at a low temperature but lasted a long time; dried cotton stems which were faster to burn, and dry manure mixed with straw which burned very fast and gave out a great deal of heat. The amount of heat was adjusted by mixing different proportions of those three substances. Regular bread needed high heat, biscuits and cakes much less.

The most fun for us kids was to be given the chance to make different shapes of biscuits such as little cars, children, men, women, stars, and others. Those were baked at the end of the day. The oven usually stayed hot long after the regular baking was finished. My mother would put a large pot with lamb, potatoes and tomatoes or a pot of fish and borghol (unripe wheat) in the oven for an hour. These were really delicious. Peasants in the countryside, who baked regularly, often slept on the warm top of the oven in the winter rather than sleeping on the floor.

Because we had no refrigeration, cheese and butter had to go through special processes to last many months without spoiling. Here came the role of the cheese lady. We could use milk or butter from cows or water buffaloes. We always chose the latter. Its milk had more fat which was good for both cheese and butter's taste. The best seasons for rich milk with heavy cream were winter and spring. The butter-melting day was special.

The lady would bring a hundred pounds of buffalo butter. It was put into two or three large pots on the stove for several hours. It kept boiling, thus becoming more and more concentrated. It was then left overnight to cool down and then stored in large glazed pots. It could last a whole year without becoming rancid. That melted butter, called "samna," was fully-saturated fat.

I guess it must have contributed to many clogged arteries and early deaths, though it gave food and cakes a distinctly delicious flavor. I have fond memories of those special occasions. The butter-melting gave such a strong aroma that we could smell it a block away.

The same woman would bring newly made soft cheese, about twenty pounds at a time. We would wrap large pieces of cheese, about three pounds each, in a special porous bamboo sheet and soak it in very salty water. The cheese lost a great deal of water and became firmer, usually dropping to two pounds. In two or three weeks, we usually had enough cheese to last until the next season. This, too, was kept in large glazed pots with a capacity of fifty pounds each, or in a square tin bucket of the same volume. These tin buckets were soldered shut until they were needed. Each house had a special storage room for year-round foods such as cheese, samna, rice, lentils, beans, honey and others.

A woman uses a wood-burning oven to bake bread.

Chapter 11
TRANSPORTATION IN BENI SUEF

When I was growing up in Beni Suef we had no public transportation. The city was crowded but its area was small. People walked to work. Children walked to school. All recreational facilities, stores and markets, were easily reachable on foot. However, there were situations where some method of transportation was necessary.

The most commonly used in-town transportation was the horse-drawn carriage. Usually, only well-to-do people used them except for special situations. Some men and many women used carriages when it was too hot to walk, as temperatures reached 105 degrees Fahrenheit or more during some summer days. No woman wanted to go to her destination sweaty with her face lotions dripping with running mascara. Carriages were also used on rainy days, which were not frequent south of Cairo.

The carriage owners' business mostly came from people traveling to or from the train station. Many travelers had heavy suitcases, or had small children traveling with them. There were two central locations for the carriages to be found. One was at the railroad station where several drivers would stand by close to the time when trains were scheduled to arrive. There were about ten trains a day going south, and a similar number going north. The first was about 5 a.m. and the last was around 11 p.m. The other carriage stand was in the center of town in the government square.

There were no more than thirty carriages in Beni Suef. We got to know the drivers by name and the color of their horse. The drivers took pride in the cleanliness of their carriages and their horses. It was so much fun to watch the horses getting a bath in the river at dusk. The driver would unhook the horse and lead it to a shallow spot used by all the drivers because it had no strong current. He would take his clothes off except for his underwear and go in with the horse. The water usually reached the horse's underbelly. The driver would lather it with a soapy cloth and then rinse the horse off with a large bucket. He usually did this to himself, too, before getting the horse dried with a large towel and hooking it back onto the carriage.

Those carriages had canopies which were up during the day for protection from the sun and down in the evening to let the cool air pass through. There was also a horizontal metal bar behind the back of the carriage about one foot off the street. I don't remember what it was for but I know it was the most fun part of the carriage for little boys. We learned to jump on quietly and sit on it facing backward, and stretched our legs out so they didn't drag or hit the many bumps on the road. We enjoyed getting a free ride. Sometimes two or three kids would ride at a time. We were careful not to make a noise. Occasionally the driver would sense that some unwanted and non-paying passengers were on his cart. He used his long whip on us. Often some jealous boys on the street would shout to the driver, "Hey, there are boys behind you!" That long whip would flick back to reach our stretched-out legs. It was painful. After the first whip we'd jump off. We learned to jump on and off the slow moving carriages without getting injured.

There were very few private cars, no more than twenty. They were owned by the rich or those in power such as the mayor, whose license number was always Beni Suef 1. Taxis were mostly used for travel between towns. There was a special stand for out of town destinations. Most of the taxis were old 1930s Fords with a high top. They had a long metal piece, a running board, on each side for passengers to step up or down to get into the car, especially for women with long dresses and children. The taxi driver had to have enough passengers on board before taking off, to make a decent living. Sometimes people had to wait half an hour until the cab was full for whatever destination. Five people usually sat on the inside leather seats and paid according to the distance to their destination. One could also stand on the metal steps on the outside of the taxi and hold on to the top rack of the taxi where suitcases were often loaded. This mode was only used by men and at a reduced fare. With poor roads, taxis were never fast enough to pose any threat to falling off, but bumps or pot holes could. One had to hold on tightly to the metal rack.

The common form of transportation in Beni Suef.

For some reason unknown to me, there was a traffic police station on the highways every now and then about fifteen to twenty miles apart, or at the entrance to small towns. These stations were basically small wooden shacks. A policeman sat outside to register all commercial vehicles passing by. Private cars were not stopped. However, taxis and buses were. When a taxi stopped, the policeman checked the driver's license, the car registration, and the number of passengers, which should not exceed the taxi's capacity. Here comes the funny part. There were often several men hanging on outside the taxi which would be a reason for citing the cab driver. To get around it, the men disembarked a hundred yards before the taxi reached the police stop and began walking along the road. After the driver passed through he'd stop a hundred yards away and wait for the walking passengers to get back on. It was a sham. The drivers knew it, the policemen knew it, and the passengers knew it, but it was technically legal. I wonder if those policemen received a little bribe from the taxi drivers to turn a blind eye?

Fords were the main commercial transportation between towns.

Buses were few and were used only for long distance travel between cities and towns. One that our family used often was the bus to Cairo where both my parents' families lived and where we often spent part of the summer vacation. Those seventy miles from Beni Suef to Cairo on a bus were an adventure by itself.

We often took the 8 a.m. bus from the depot. As there was only one bus every two hours to Cairo, it could fill up fast. We needed reservations. My father would give me some money and I would go to the depot at 6 a.m. to pay a deposit and inform them of the number of seats required. The first four rows on the bus were considered first class and were more expensive than the back seats. We always rode first class. Then I would go to the horse-driven carriage stand and reserve one carriage to come to our house at seven a.m. Mission accomplished, I'd return home. By 7 a.m. the suitcases were packed and ready, and us kids excited and anxious for the trip. My parents would make sure that all the windows in the house were closed, the lights were off, the kitchen was clean, and the garbage put out. We gave a key to a neighbor to check on the house and feed the chickens on the rooftop.

When the carriage arrived, the kids, my mom, and the suitcases were piled on. If there was not enough space in the carriage, the older kids walked to the bus depot. My father always sat in the front seat on the bus behind the driver. They talked all the time telling stories and jokes. It was fun to pass by villages, watching women carrying water from the Nile in large jars on their heads, a boy pulling a buffalo to the farm, or just the trees on the side of the road as they passed by.

The buses were slow. It could take four or more hours to get to Cairo but very few people were in a hurry. We often passed farmers' markets in villages. They always had fresh produce at reasonable prices. The driver would stop and ask the passengers if they wanted to buy anything. Usually we did. It could take ten to twenty minutes before starting to get driving again. The driver would also stop if a kid wanted to go to the bathroom. There were always outdoor cafes at many villages and small towns willing to help. On very hot days, some passengers would disembark to buy ice-cold Coca-Cola in those little fancy bottles.

However, there was a limit to any delays. In one incident, as we were returning from Cairo in the evening, we passed as usual by a small town. The driver announced that he was stopping for half an hour to attend a wedding of a relative's daughter. The passengers were annoyed as it could be much longer than half an hour. My father, who was sitting immediately behind the driver, grabbed the back of the driver's shirt and threatened to report him to the authorities, which meant he'd get fired. The driver only stopped for ten minutes to offer his congratulations to the bride and groom.

Beni Suef, like most Egyptian cities, was linked by rail, built with the help of the British in the late nineteenth century. The rails were laid so that trains would go on the left as it was in Britain. Driving cars however, was on the right side as most of the cars were made in America or Germany early on. The trains were coal burning, with billowing smoke, but were much faster than buses. The trip to Cairo only took two hours on the express train with a handful of stops, and two and half hours on all others.

There were three classes on most trains. First and second class seats were in compartments which seated eight people, had leather seats, and a rack for suitcases. I don't remember if there was air conditioning or not, or what the differences were between first and second classes, as I always rode in third class. The seats were wood and the windows had to remain open to bring in fresh air which also brought black soot inside. On long trips passengers' faces were blackened. But the price was right. Trains were almost always crowded. There would be as many people standing as sitting. Every now and then a conductor passed through to inspect the tickets. Those who didn't have a ticket had to pay a penalty.

Some young men preferred to ride free. They jumped on top of the trains and lay on their stomach to avoid decapitation when the train passed under a bridge. Others hung outside the train holding onto the edge of the open windows. The conductors paid no attention to them, leaving them to fate. Occasionally, after the conductor passed through a car, the inside passengers pulled in the outside hangers-on for their safety and out of compassion. I do not know how many people got hurt or even killed this way.

The slow or so-called local trains were the lifeline of high school students from villages and small towns. Beni Suef, being the capital of a province, had the only high school for girls for 30 miles in each direction and ten miles for boys. The 7 a.m. train was always full of teenagers coming to school on weekdays, and so was the 4 p.m. train. I was fortunate to have lived in a city where our high school was only a twenty-minute walk away. The country kids had long days, especially in the winter. They could easily leave their house in the dark and return in the dark.

There were one or two very fast trains called Pullmans, which were said to run by electricity and not coal. They had no third class seats and were much more expensive. They stopped only at provincial capitals and were used only by wealthy people, businessmen, or tourists heading south to Luxor. Those trains took only one and a half hours to or from Cairo to Beni Suef with only one stop in between, the city of Giza, where the pyramids are.

On many trains, especially long distances, many people in third class brought their own food, filling the air with its aroma. But there was always a man walking through, selling tea, coffee and sandwiches. At each train stop vendors crowded the platform selling many foods, fruit, and soft drinks which people bought through the open windows.

Beni Suef lacked many specialty stores. That led to the presence of a man we knew as the roving salesman. People would go to his house to place orders for whatever they wanted him to buy for them in Cairo. It could be cloth material of a certain color or quality, small electrical appliances, or other items. He took the 8 a.m. train to Cairo and returned on the 6 p.m. train. After arriving in Cairo, he roamed downtown, buying whatever was requested that day, and return with multiple large suitcases. He did that job six days a week. He was the lifeline for hundreds of families needing Cairo's merchandise. When business boomed after the end of World War II, his two sons joined him. The small fee we paid was worth it as he knew exactly where the good and reasonable stuff in Cairo was available.

Freight trains were the lifeline of all commerce. They replaced the Nile river shipping. It would take forever for freight trains to pass by. I had a friend whose house was adjacent to the railroad tracks. It was fun to count the number of cars the trains pulled. The highest number was seventy- six. Many towns and city stations had extra side railroad tracks. The freight trains often diverted to them, to let faster scheduled passenger trains pass on the main track, before resuming their journey.

The country train was fun. It was always noisy but entertaining to watch. The peasants let us pet their animals. The habitable land in Beni Suef was only fifteen miles around the Nile. Beyond the fifteen miles was the desert. On that narrow strip of land many villages thrived. There were no paved roads in most of them. Country trains, slow as they were, became good alternatives to the donkey for the movement of people and goods. It was also very useful for peasants to bring their produce to town but the trains were so slow that one could jog past it! Peasants could flag it to stop anywhere between villages. Many people brought small animals on board such as goats, sheep or ducks for the city market.

There was a small church at the end of that country line. I occasionally went with some boys to the church on Sundays during summer holidays. The train ride was an adventure by itself. There was only one train with no fixed schedule and one railroad track. It made slow round trips from sunrise to sunset.

Other modes of transportation were available but used less and less over time. They included the donkey and the donkey-driven flat wooden cart, which many peasants rode, especially women visiting a relative or a friend in a hospital. These of course were very slow, but very few people were in a hurry those days. Bicycles and motorcycles were rarely used as most people could not afford them.

Chapter 12
COMMUNICATION IN EGYPT

Egypt, the land of the pyramids, had a pyramidal system for many aspects of life, in government, religion, and communication among other things. Everything flowed from Cairo downward. Those in power talked. Others simply listened.

Up to the mid-1950s, there was only one radio station in the whole country, controlled by the government and located in Cairo. Its staff was employed by the government. Personal opinions had no place unless they were supportive of whichever government was in power.

The broadcast aired at certain times of the day and the segments were programmatically set. It started at 6 a.m. with the reciting of the Koran and ended around midnight the same way. On special occasions, such as the month of Ramadan, and often on Thursday nights when there was a live broadcast of famous singers, it lasted much longer. Whenever the time came for one of the five Muslim prayers during the day, the regular broadcasts stopped and the voice of a muezzin called people to prayer.

There were three regular periods of broadcast: 6 a.m. to 10:30 a.m., noon to 3 p.m. and 5 p.m. to midnight. There was always news, songs, and the stock market. The news usually started with what the prime minister did or said, followed by lesser government personnel. There was mostly good news of what was to be done for the people. The economy was always improving, according to the news, no matter what the common people saw on the street.

Only well-to-do people during World War II had radios. Radios in those days could not run on batteries, so houses with no electricity had no use for radios. Radios were mostly German made. Ours was a huge Grundig, which weighed over forty pounds, and was put high up on a heavy and sturdy shelf that only adults could reach. My imagination at age two or three, or whenever I first heard the radio, was that little people talked within, and the reason the radio was not on all the time, was that those little people needed rest like we did.

A German radio from 1930s.

Many children in the neighborhood had no radio. Our radio was on most of the time. When there was a nice song they wanted to hear, I would ask my mom to turn the radio louder as the neighbor kids sat under our open windows to listen. I was told that I had a musical ear and was very good at memorizing. I learned many songs and would be singing to my mom while helping her in the noisy kitchen where two or three kerosene stoves would be on.

The radio also broadcast news of very important events in the country such as the progress of the Cholera epidemic, or the Nile flood, or other calamities of a large scale. Individual accidents, crimes, or local news were not aired unless a very important person was involved. The best thing for us, other than songs and jokes, was the live broadcast of rival soccer teams on Fridays, the weekly holiday, from Cairo. Most people took sides, cheered, or booed as the announcer yelled out the play by play. Only large cities had soccer teams. Beni Suef had none.

The cafes downtown had their radios at full blast during all broadcasting times so that the noisy customers could hear. The passersby could hear too. It made that part of the city lively. All buildings in that area were either commercial or governmental with no residential housing, so the music, even at midnight, would not bother homes and their sleeping occupants far away.

The radio was our lifeline to the outside world. I got to know who Churchill and Roosevelt were at age six. The progress of World War II was continuously broadcast. When a very important official died, all singing stopped and it was replaced with reciting the Koran for hours. It was through the radio that we heard of the abdication of King Farouk, the death of Stalin, and the nationalization of banks by Nasser. It also broadcasted Nasser's three hour speeches on many occasions. Until I left Egypt in May 1959, there was no television. It was introduced a year later.

Local news spread from person to person. With narrow streets, open windows and balconies, and women at home all day, it did not take long for anything, especially juicy stories, death, or a new baby's birth to move across town. The average house did not have a phone. Only high government officials, professionals, commercial establishments, and hospitals did. Many corner stores had phones for the public to use for a small fee. There was no direct dialing. One called the operator and gave the name. The male operators would connect the caller. There was a central telephone and telegram office in downtown Beni Suef. Calls to Cairo or other cities had to be initiated there. Telegrams were used more often than telephones, mainly for congratulations, condolences and the like. Telegrams were delivered to the homes day and night.

There was very little mail and no bills, as people paid in cash. They kept their meager savings, if any, at home. If they put money in a bank, they had to go in person during banking hours to make a deposit. The most common use of mail was family correspondence. When a young man went to a university or to work in another town, the mail was the lifeline with his family. Single girls who worked stayed in their home town with very few exceptions.

The busiest time for the mailman was around Christmas and Easter when Christians from different towns exchanged cards. There were no mail collection boxes, and no mail delivery boxes. Mail was delivered in person. If no one was home, the mailman might give the letter to a neighbor to deliver it. We had to go to the post office downtown to buy stamps and deposit the letters. People who got letters frequently became well known to the postman, who kept his job for life unless promoted. Letters could be delivered to those people even if there was no correct address written. Regular letters needed what is equal to a one cent stamp. After World War II it rose to two cents. Telegrams were 25 cents or more depending on the length of the message.

There were, however, many newspapers, all printed in Cairo. Before Nasser's time, there were many political parties, each of which had its own newspaper, some daily, some weekly. New parties often arose, others split or combined. The number of newspapers changed periodically. The premier newspaper was called "Alahram," meaning "The Pyramids," and was established in 1875, before there were even political parties during the Ottoman Empire control of Egypt. It was, and still is, the most widely circulated daily newspaper in Egypt.

Like other papers, it published government, national and international news. Its commentary, however, was non-partisan. Its most famous section was the obituaries for the whole country. With few phones and limited access to telegrams, families and friends from different parts of Egypt only learned about the death of someone through the Alahram. It was the first few pages that older men read in the morning. Burial in Egypt was not to exceed twenty-four hours after a person's death, for health reasons and religious customs. If one knew the time and place of the funeral that day, he would attend, or send a telegram if far away.

There was no such thing as a free press. A government employee was assigned to each newspaper to oversee that material, especially the commentary section. One could criticize state ministers but not the king. After the 1952 revolution, when Egypt became a republic, censorship became even worse, and covered all government actions during Nasser's reign. Sadat and Mubarak eased censoring, except for themselves and their families.

The distribution of the daily newspaper was amazing. The early edition was printed by 2 a.m. A special carriage in the 3 a.m. train from Cairo to Aswan was dedicated to carrying newspapers and magazines. The papers were bundled with the names of the towns and cities that train would pass by, as the express train didn't stop, except in provincial capitals. The newspaper bundles were thrown out onto the platforms at the precise moment the train passed by. This way, all the papers were delivered, even to Aswan, 500 miles south of Cairo before noon. The train passed by Beni Suef at 5 a.m. So we received our newspapers early. Many people read the paper before they went to work, or took it with them to their government offices where they read and discussed the news when work was slow.

In 1947, two well-known newspaper men, Ali and Mostafa Amin, who were twins, visited several European countries as well as the U.S. to get familiar with advanced methods of publishing. They returned a few months later with several ideas that revolutionized Egyptian newspapers. They started a new paper called the "Daily News" where the emphasis was not on government or politics but on social issues, people, crime, gossip and stories of personal interest.

The author's mother in 1956.

It flourished and surpassed most papers' distribution in a short time. They also suggested a celebration day for all the mothers of Egypt in recognition as the unsung heroines of society. Thus, in the 1950s, Mother's Day was first celebrated in Egypt. The first day of spring, March 21st, was chosen to be Mother's Day. Songs were written with beautiful lyrics and music, and sung by the best singers of the time. Those songs brought tears to my eyes, and still do when I hear them.

We were not rich enough to buy expensive gifts for mom from our allowance. My father had so many expenses that we did not dare ask him for extra money. I suggested to my brothers and sisters that we pool our allowances and take mom to the local photographer for a small portrait. She was pleased, put on a pretty dress, fixed her hair nice, and got her picture taken. It was a hit. We did this every year thereafter until I left Egypt a few years later. Those annual pictures are a treasure and a reminder of the gentle soul who raised us.

After World War II many weekly and monthly magazines came into being. Some flourished and some folded. They were specialty magazines, such as sports, movie stars, comics, women's, children's, and several about social life in Egypt, especially the rich and famous. No one could afford all those very interesting publications. After reading a magazine, people would sell them for a penny each to a salesman who passed by once a week. They were spread on the stone fence of a well-known park to be sold for a few pennies each. It was good business for everyone. I used to buy Reader's Digest in Arabic and English of the same issue when I was in high school. I would read them and learn new words. It helped me become the best student in English, and gave me a glimpse of life in America. Subconsciously, this might have been one of my reasons for longing to go to America, a dream that I fulfilled many years later.

Chapter 13
ENTERTAINMENT

When I was growing up in Beni Suef in the 1940s, and in Cairo in the 1950s, television had not yet arrived in Egypt. It was introduced in 1960 after I left the country. In Beni Suef, there were few entertainment venues, but we enjoyed them. In Cairo there were dozens of theatrical outlets, most of which we could not afford. Most families had five to ten children and it would be beyond reason to spend so much money throughout the year for such activities

Middle-class people never bought toys for their children. The limited income they had was spent on shelter, food and education. Children made their own toys. We used clay to make figures of animals, birds and people. We also used mud mixed with small pieces of straw to build cars, houses, boats, and other things and set them out to dry in the sun. The more elaborate toys were dolls made by my mother from scraps of material. The shape was first drawn on paper, then cut out in fabric, stitched together, and filled with cotton or pieces of old worn out clothes or socks.

Birthday celebrations were unheard of. The only person whose birthday we celebrated was King Farouk's, which was a national holiday for schools and government offices. No programs, just a day off in late January each year. The happiest though modest celebration was graduation from High School, where neighbors visited the house of the successful student and offered "sharbat," sweetened fruit juice, but no cakes.

The first birthday party I witnessed was when I started medical school in Cairo. The Gray's Anatomy textbook was too expensive for my father to afford, but was necessary to have. A rich friend of my father in Beni Suef had a son in medical school in Cairo who was about to graduate. He offered to give my father his son's Gray's Anatomy for free. I was relieved and ecstatic. I had to go to the son's house in an upscale area in Cairo. One evening I took the tram to pick up the book. As I approached the large apartment I heard loud music. I knocked on the door, and to my surprise there were at least a dozen young men drinking wine and swaying to the tunes. I wondered if they were preparing for a groom's night before a wedding. The person who escorted me laughed.

"Today we are celebrating the birthday of one of the young men," he said.

I guess if someone had extra money to spend, that was their business. I did not stay. I received the anatomy book and hurried home to study.

There was only one movie theater in Beni Suef used throughout the year. During the summers it was open air to allow for summer breezes as there was no air conditioning. In the cool winter months a canopy was erected, about twenty feet high, to keep people warm. There was one show every night, starting after dusk and lasting about three hours. It always began with announcements of future movies, and a few advertisements from big retail companies about their merchandise. Between 1940 and 1945 a short segment in English with Arabic subtitles was also shown about the progress of the World War II, with Churchill, Roosevelt, General Montgomery and other army officials. It always portrayed the Western Alliance as victorious.

There were both American and Egyptian movies. The Egyptian movies were more fun as we understood easily what was happening. They were full of singing and belly dancing. The American movies, however, were more exciting. With Arabic subtitles we got the idea of what was being said as it was hard to follow the rapid speech of the actors' different accents. What intrigued me most were the beautiful scenery, the elaborate stories, the sophisticated actors, and the obvious richness of Hollywood. In my fantasy I wished I could someday visit America.

The movie, no matter how long or short, was divided into two sections with a half-hour intermission where salesmen walked around selling Coca-Cola or other drinks in addition to roasted corn on the cob. The first class ticket holders sat on cushioned chairs in the back part of the theater and could also buy French pastries.

Advertising what was playing in the theater that day was an interesting event in town. Around 3 p.m. a flat wooden cart, pulled by a donkey, paraded along the main streets. Two large eight feet by eight feet boards were mounted on the cart in a pyramid shape displaying huge paper posters of the name of the movie and pictures of the main characters. Thus, people on both sides of the street would see it. Walking ahead of the cart were two or three men playing brass instruments. Once people heard the music from a block or two away they came out to their balconies or to their windows to see what was playing that day.

During the summer of 1944, a free outdoor cinema was set up in a large park next to the River Nile on Thursday nights. People flocked there from all over the city, bringing blankets to sit on in the grassy area, and sandwiches. Coca-Cola was available for sale, providing a great family picnic while watching a movie for free. However, for some reason it only lasted one summer.

The radio broadcasted the news three times a day and began with the playing of the triumphant march from the opera "Aida." All the singing was in Arabic. Many singers became famous through radio broadcasts. The most famous singer of my generation was a lady named "Om Kolthom." She had an amazing voice, was well versed in classical Arabic, and chose her own lyrics from the multitude of writers and musicians clamoring to work with her. Her melodies and voice were superb. Her songs were almost always about lost love, and lasted one hour each. She performed alone once a month in a large theater in Cairo attended by the rich, the famous and the powerful, including King Farouk and later President Nasser. During her performances on the first Thursday of the month, everything stopped. The radio broadcast her three songs from 10 p.m. until 2 a.m. Cafes in Beni Suef were full of men listening to her, while families with children listened at home. When she had a thyroid problem in the 1950s, President Eisenhower invited her to be treated with the then-new radioisotope procedure in a military hospital in Washington, D.C.

Om Kolthom toured the Arab capitals from Beirut to Morocco. Her shows brought in much-needed hard currency to Egypt. Her career lasted from 1925 to 1975. She was, and still is, the most loved and respected singer of the twentieth century in the Middle East. Her songs continue to bring joy and tranquility to this day, with hundreds of aspiring singers imitating her style.

There were many other great singers in that golden age of music in Egypt but none like her.

Once a year, a famous circus came from Cairo for one week. A huge tent was erected in a large square for its shows. The admission price was affordable and the shows were great. It included the usual attractions of dancing elephants and horses, tight-rope walkers, playful monkeys, clowns, acrobats, and the taming of tigers. We children enjoyed the show as well as eating cotton candy. My parents paid for it all. There were also swings outside the tent costing one penny for ten minutes, which we paid for ourselves from our allowance.

In Cairo, where I moved to attend medical school in September 1951, there were numerous theaters for live shows in addition to the movie theaters. These included musicals, comedies, dramas, and variety shows. I attended only a few during my medical school years for lack of time and money. But during my internship year, 1958 to 1959, I attended many more. It was a thrill to see singers in person whom I'd enjoyed listening to on the radio for many years. I also enjoyed theatrical plays, especially comedies.

Whether in Beni Suef, or Cairo, I enjoyed movies, the theater, and entertainment in general. They provided a well-balanced life that added joy to my busy years as a student.

Chapter 14
SIZE, HORMONES AND UNDERWEAR

I was a precocious kid, which was a mixed blessing. Intellectually and hormonally I was ahead of children my age. I learned fast, had a good memory, was overactive, and wanted to know everything about everything. My parents encouraged me, my older brothers helped me, and my teachers pushed me to excel with high praise. I could not have asked for more. I was always two years younger than the average pupil in the class. I enrolled in first grade at four years and ten months old and skipped second grade. So, I received my primary grade, (seventh grade) certificate at age ten years and eight months and high school (twelfth grade) at fifteen years and eight months.

I was always the shortest kid in the class at every grade. People thought I was younger than my real age because of my size. They were surprised to know which grade I was in and I enjoyed seeing the astonishment on their faces. My arms and legs were even shorter in comparison to the rest of my body, which was already short. Desks in classrooms were designed for the average size child for that grade. Being smaller, with even shorter legs, I was never able to put my feet on the floor while sitting. My legs were always dangling, often moving rhythmically as if being exercised at all times.

Boys were seated in the classroom by size, so I was always in the first row. That was an advantage and a disadvantage. I could clearly see the blackboard which was the center for information as the teachers always wrote on it while we copied the lessons. There were no visual aids. But I was always right under the teacher's nose so I couldn't goof off. However, I often showed my boredom by the speed at which my legs moved.

My small size made me unable to compete in sports with other boys from the same grade on school grounds, while my pride prevented me from playing with kids my size in lower grades. I spent a great deal of my lunch time reading under the many shady trees. Fortunately for me, the sports played in the street had nothing to do with school grades, neither was the children's sports club program at church. In these two venues, I fitted in and excelled because of my agility, speed, good muscle coordination, and endurance. I was always first pick in choosing players for the soccer teams. I was good at racket tennis, and reasonable at volleyball and table tennis, but I never played basketball or tried wrestling.

Because of my size I was the target of jokes by my classmates. I remember that I weighed fifty pounds in seventh grade and was fifty inches tall. I heard it all. At first it bothered me but later I learned some comebacks. After all, I was the undisputed top student in academics in every class. When I was really irritated, I'd say, "What counts is what is above the neck and in this I am ahead of you!"

That would shut them up.

One embarrassing event happened in the ninth grade. The school had a new gatekeeper. He wouldn't let me in. I was eleven years old but looked like a nine year old. He said, "Where are you going, kid?"

He thought that I'd come to see my brother, or a teacher, or that I was just goofing off from my real school and wanted to hide on high school grounds. I told him, "I'm going to class."

I said it with great seriousness but he didn't believe me. Fortunately, several boys in my class had just walked in and saw the commotion. They told the gatekeeper that I really was a student in that school. He let me in. They made a lot of jokes about saving me but I didn't use my usual comeback responses. I was grateful to them.

Puberty also kicked in early. It was a drawback for my ultimate growth. When sex hormones reach a certain level, the ends of a human's long bones stop growing. That is where growth spurts occur. So I ended even shorter than what was anticipated. I reached five feet two inches at age fifteen and stopped at that, while my brothers reached five feet nine inches or five feet ten inches.

We learned about sexual development from older boys. They told us that nocturnal emission, whatever that was, started at age thirteen or fourteen. For me it was twelve.

There was a bright side to being short. Most clothes, including suits, were custom made. As I was small, less material was needed, thus costing less. The major benefit, however, came when I reached the age to be drafted in the army. Army life in Egypt was not pleasant. At age nineteen I had to report to the army center for a check-up. Being in college would have postponed my enlisting until after graduation. However, the physical examination showed me shorter than the five feet three inch minimum height requirement which meant that I would be permanently exempt. What a relief! I was given a certificate to that effect which was crucial to getting permission to leave the country for any male between the ages of twenty and forty years old.

In the early 1940s in Beni Suef there were very few ready-made clothes for children. Whatever was available was expensive and would only last for a short time for a growing child. Fabric, however, was plentiful. Almost all the clothes I needed were made by my mother. Only shoes, suits, and girl's fancy dresses were made by professional dressmakers. My mother sewed our shirts, pajamas, galabias, school uniforms and underwear.

The underwear for boys and girls were similar. There was no access from the front for the penis. The pants, called trousers, had buttons in front. There were no zippers then. As a boy I had to unbuckle the belt, undo the buttons and pull the trousers to mid-thigh. With no front opening in the underwear I had to pull those down too. It was a laborious task, as was putting things back in place, buttons, belt and all.

We changed our underwear twice a week, once on Thursday or Friday when we took a bath and once midweek. That was the routine during winter. We could bathe more often during summer by taking cold showers. There was no municipal hot water. Over time clothing material got worn out and became easily torn from material fatigue. One night, at the age of eleven, I must have had a strong erection. While wearing old underwear, it split at a strategic location with the penis head poking through the hole. I wanted to change it in the morning before going to school, but for some reason, during the morning rush, I forgot. It was a great day for urination! I simply pulled the penis out of the torn part with no fuss to maneuver it as usual.

I wondered what to tell my mother. After school I asked her for a change of underwear. She told me that the next day was the bathing day and with limited clothing she would agree if my underwear was dirty enough. I almost died when she volunteered to wash it herself as the woman who came to wash our clothes came on Saturdays, which was three days hence.

Knowing my mother, whether embarrassed or not, I could not say no. She looked at the underwear while my eyes were gazing at the floor. I didn't know what she was going to say. To my surprise she put her hand on my shoulder and said, "This underwear should be thrown away."

Obviously, she found the hole. I took my eyes from the floor, looked at her gratefully and said, "Give it to me. I'll make use of it."

I washed it myself. It became the core of a soccer ball which I called "the ball of manhood." I was satisfied with that happy ending. However, I was saddened to see that useful hole gone. I wondered why they didn't make an opening with buttons in the front of boy's underwear as they did with the trousers.

A few months later in early 1947 a new children's store for ready-made clothes opened in Beni Suef. World War II was over and new merchandise of all sorts started coming to town. My father bought us new underwear. It surpassed my dreams. It had no buttons, but an ingeniously designed slit that kept the penis well protected when not in use, and allowed it to easily come out when need be. The process of urination for boys took less time and was less cumbersome. The difference in anatomy between boys and girls became functional. Finally, the penis took its rightful place and well-deserved position in the daily life of boys.

Nocturnal emission was another milestone in my life. One night at age twelve, I felt a twitch in my penis. I woke up. There was an involuntary spurt of something which we were told by older boys would be like thick milk. It soiled my underwear. I immediately went to the bathroom, cleaned it up as much as I could, and returned to bed. The next day was bathing day. After taking a bath, I tossed the underwear in the hamper. I knew that the wash lady soaked the clothes in hot water before the wash, and thus the soil would not become obvious.

My emissions began to happen every couple of weeks. Other boys talked about releasing it through masturbation. Christians were told in the church that masturbation was a sin. I was a good boy but the night event didn't stop. It was not under my control. I guess it was nature's way of clearing up the old to make space for the new.

Chapter 15
SEX AND FLIRTING

Talking about sex when I was growing up was considered an abomination in public and a cherished topic in private. Egyptian society was segregated by gender. Sex before marriage was punishable by death, called "honor killing." I occasionally saw decomposed corpses floating on the water of the Nile, coming from southern Egypt. Most probably these were girls found pregnant, murdered and thrown in the river, having dishonored the name of the family. If the man who impregnated her was identified, he would be killed too.

The police turned a blind eye. No investigations of these killings were carried out. They were men too, and had daughters. They felt the same as the murdered girls' families. Some girls who got pregnant in a small town escaped murder by fleeing to Cairo, working as a servant in someone's house, and claiming that her husband had divorced or deserted her.

Schools were segregated from fourth to twelfth grade. Schools for girls in Beni Suef went only as far as ninth grade until 1945. Girls stayed home after that to help their mothers and to learn how to cook, sew, and bake while waiting for an older, well-heeled man to marry. Girls would go out either in groups or accompanied by an older brother, or a male relative. The town was safe, but the gossip was abundant. There was no violence, only the fear of a damaged reputation.

Boys, on the other hand, could go wherever and whenever they wanted. There were no jobs in the summer. Escaping hot, non-air-conditioned houses, young people flocked to the Corniche, or river shore, where there was a nice breeze. Some simply stood on street corners, talking, joking and whistling at girls as they walked by in groups.

There was no such thing as dating. Most marriages were semi-arranged between families who knew each other. However, the boy and girl had to agree, which was the norm. Even then, they could not go out together until they wore engagement rings.

Occasionally, new young people moved into town, usually for government jobs. If a couple walked together, they were frowned upon unless somebody confirmed that they were married. Young boys tried to find out by sneaking up behind them, and following them to see if they ended at separate houses. If they did, they would be harassed the next time around by boys chanting and cursing because the couple would be considered fooling around and deserved to be punished.

Men and women, even a husband and wife, didn't hold hands, or, God forbid, kissed in public. However, two men or women could walk around holding hands as a sign of friendship. Sometimes young men put their arms on each other's shoulder. If they met after a long absence, they hugged. They often rubbed cheek to cheek but never kissed.

When women hugged each other, which happened every time they met, they kissed in the air while the two right or two left cheeks were touching. No kisses on the lips. If a woman didn't hug another when they met, it was considered a snub and an insult. Usually, however, upper-class women didn't hug lower class women, but greeted them verbally.

Profanity in the streets, away from our families' ears, was common. We used sexual and derogatory words about each other. The utmost insult would be mentioning the private parts of a boy's mother or sister. This could be the beginning of a bloody war. If a boy was unable to deal with it he would call on the neighbors' kids who would rush over in droves to punish the insulting boy. Kids often threw stones from a distance, or had fist fights. However, there was never a use of knives or guns which were not allowed for civilian citizens. There were many bruises, but rarely a cut and almost never a broken bone.

Not being able to talk about town girls they knew, boys talked about the sex lives of women we would never meet, such as movie stars or glamorous belly dancers. You'd never read a sexual joke in a newspaper. These kinds of jokes were passed along verbally from person to person.

The greatest outlet, however, was in the movie house. There was only one in town and it operated all year. There were three classes of seats, each with a different price. For five cents one could purchase a third class ticket and sit on wooden benches in the very front, with no back support. Second class was at a little higher level at ten cents and was mostly for poor families. First class was twenty-five cents for the rich. They sat on comfortable chairs and could buy food during intermission.

The third class area was mostly for boys and young men. We liked to watch American movies. Some of us learned English in school, but the slang and dialect was hard to understand so we depended on the Arabic subtitles. There were certainly situations and scenes in the movies where language wasn't needed. We preferred American movies to Arabic movies because American men were better kissers. When the hero kissed the lady, especially if it was a long kiss, the whole third class audience would clap and whistle and urge him to do more. If a villain approached from behind, the crowd screamed, warning the hero to watch out, as if he could hear us. The atmosphere was jovial and raucous. It allowed boys and young men to live in a fantasy world, filling our emotional vacuum, and was the closest thing to satisfying our sexual desires. Yes, we lived in a fantasy world. A lot of talk, but little action. Our main outlet was Hollywood.

As we were not able to talk about sex with girls or women, homosexual talk was common. In Arabic there is no such word as "gay." Instead, we used two very different words. The top man, so to speak, is literally called a "boy's man" and is frowned upon. The bottom man has a different word, which is equivalent to "queer" or "fag." Under Islamic Sharia Law, he is to be punished by death. No one that we knew in our town was so described. If they were, they must have hidden it completely or moved to one of the two cosmopolitan cities in Egypt, namely Cairo and Alexandria.

Boys bragged about how macho they were, especially when their voices started to change. I'll never forget an incident that happened in seventh grade. The classrooms usually measured about thirty feet by thirty feet. There were four double desks in each of five rows. The maximum number of students was forty, but usually much fewer. Each desk had two large drawers where we kept our books and other school supplies. Two students sat at each desk. Shorter boys sat in the front row, the rest sat in succession by height, so the big boys were always in the back of the classroom. They were usually much older and less inclined academically, as many of them had repeated some grades over the years. When I was ten years old, the oldest boy in my class was seventeen, but most were thirteen or fourteen.

The teachers spent a great deal of time writing on the blackboard while we copied the words into our notebooks. The boys in the back were always goofing off, chatting and clowning around whenever the teacher turned his back. Every now and then he would turn around and order us to be quiet but classrooms were never really quiet. Most schools were located on noisy main streets with the windows open during summer months.

One day while the teacher was writing, I heard the sound "wow" followed by giggles. The teacher turned and scolded us. We kept silent until he started writing again. Suddenly there was a louder "wow." The teacher scolded us again. At the end of the period, the boys in front inquired from the boys in the back about what was going on. One boy, we were told, opened the buttons of his pants and showed his seatmate his erect penis. That was the first "Wow!" Then an older boy behind him did the same and stood up to show the boys on both sides of his desk his "tool." Hence the louder "Wow!"

There were frequent rumors of homosexual acts among some students but none were really confirmed. One such story was of a rich boy in class who had an expensive camera and printed great pictures. He was fourteen years old, handsome, and well dressed. The rumor was that he frequented a photo shop owned by an unmarried man in his thirties. The man, we were told, did the printing in the dark room of his studio accompanied by the boy, having sex with him in exchange for his special work.

Another rumor concerned a well-to-do boy who was an excellent art student. The art teacher was a man in his late twenties who obviously favored the boy for his excellent work. The teacher came to the school on Fridays, which was the weekly holiday in Egypt, to correct the homework of the 200 students from various classes to whom he taught art. Rumor had it that the student in question came to the school on Fridays and spent some time alone with the teacher. What went on between them was left to our imagination. Several students decided to stalk them the following year to find the truth. Unfortunately for them, the boy's father, who was a government employee, was transferred to another city during the summer. Nobody will ever know the truth.

One wonders whether these stories were made up by less affluent boys who were jealous of those with wealth, as a defense mechanism for their poverty, or to fill their fantasies with made-up stories of kids they didn't like.

Regardless of the truth, the conversations were juicy and filled some empty heads with laughter.

Even Egyptian male singers didn't refer to their love objects with the feminine pronoun, but with the male. When one listens to love songs in Arabic from the 1940s, one gets the impression that all male singers were homosexual, describing love to him. Fortunately, this has changed over the years. Literature, however, which depicts love both in Arabic or English, tells stories of love between men and women, sometimes in great detail, but without explicit language. These novels were eagerly read by every one of all ages, again filling the vacuum of reality.

The school yard was continuously surveyed by the school sergeant, especially the bathrooms. Every now and then he would enter to ensure that no one was smoking or loitering. Students were not allowed to use the bathroom except during recess time, or if someone had a medical problem as per a physician's report. The bathrooms were always crowded as there were very few urinals for several hundred boys. I doubt anything happened there with ten or more boys present at any given time.

However, the situation changed drastically when students went to live in Cairo to attend University. They lived in rentals, away from family or curious neighbors. Prostitutes were the main source of sexual activities for these young men. Other girls were not an option. There were no birth control pills, condoms were unheard of, and everyone knew that pregnancy would doom a girl's life. Abortion was dangerous and only carried out in dark and unsanitary places. A non-virgin would never find a respectable man. If deceived and it was discovered that his bride was not a virgin, the man had legal cause for annulment for both Muslims and Christian Egyptians, under the claim of fraud.

Sexual harassment was not in our vocabulary in the 1950s in Egypt. It was called flirtation and was not only acceptable but even expected and occasionally invited.

Boys often talked about their conquests with girls, but no names were ever mentioned. In large families, every girl would have a brother or a male cousin who considered himself the guardian of their chastity. The next best way to express their sexual desires was for young people, who were idle throughout the summer as there was no such thing as summer jobs, to congregate on street corners and talk. The summer heat brought most people outside their homes, walking and socializing by the banks of the Nile, enjoying the gentle wind and coolness of being close to the river.

In town, girls always walked in groups on the other side of the narrow streets from the congregating boys to avoid eye contact. When the girls were nearby, the boys would whistle and compliment them on their beauty with some sexual innuendo in their voice and gestures. Girls giggled but kept moving. Such comments from boys were expected. Occasionally a boy would single out one of the girls with his comments such as, "Honey, you with the red dress. Would you like to hold my hand?"

She would not, of course, respond but the other girls would be envious and wondered if they might be less desirable or less pretty in the eyes of the boys.

Another kind of flirtation occurred within nearby houses. Many people in the summer sat on their balconies or by open windows to enjoy the fresh air. With narrow streets and overhanging balconies, the view of each other was clear and the voices easily heard. However the balconies were not a place of choice for flirtation. Passersby would see them and promptly report the action to the girl's family for possible punishment.

The favorite spot was about three feet back from an open window. Communication was a sort of pantomime. The boy threw kisses in the air towards the girl. She might reciprocate if interested, or might move away from the window if not. More often however, she would just stand there, enjoying the summer breeze and the flying kisses. Her family members, whether parents, siblings or grandparents, would see nothing and suspect nothing unless one of them wanted to stand by the window. In that case, the girl or the boy would retreat inside the house, thus ending the imaginary love session.

The ultimate in sexual harassment occurred in Cairo on the buses, but not in the small city of Beni Suef. The buses were always crowded, with more people standing than sitting. There could be a hundred passengers on a fifty-seat bus during rush hour. There were two seats on each side, with ample poles and hanging leather straps to hold on to in the middle. The passengers were generally kind, allowing older or pregnant women to have a seat. Young men or even women would give up their seats to those who were less healthy or with small children.

The roads were never smooth in most areas. As the bus sped up, slowed down for a stop, or turned a corner, people who were standing would sway and occasionally lose their balance. Some men enjoyed the sway by rubbing against the person in front of them.

Some men, if they took the bus at the beginning of its route, would deliberately sit on the aisle seat, even though the window seat might be vacant. They hoped for a gorgeous female to sit next to them. When the opportunity arose and while the woman was passing by him to get to the window seat, he'd stretch out his arm, holding it against the back of the seat with his palm facing forward. The woman sat, often ignoring his hand touching her back, grateful that she could sit.

As the bus moved, so did the man's hand, gently caressing the woman's back. If there was a loud objection from the woman, he would apologize and take his arm away completely. If she didn't react, his hand kept going down slowly till it reached the seat. Some women protested, others suffered in silence, while a few might have enjoyed the free massage. On the buses girls could not escape these occasional encounters but the situation was different on the tram or Metro, as they had small compartments for women only.

On the buses, standing passengers continuously rubbed their bodies against each other, providing some men with an excellent opportunity for sexual gratification. With no sexual outlet for most young men, a few rubs could cause immediate arousal. The more the bus swayed the more erect penises there would be. Those wearing a galabia had an easier time with this than those wearing pants which restricted their pleasure. It didn't matter for those aroused whether they rubbed against the front or the back of a woman or even a man. It was as close as they could get to another person's flesh without having to apologize.

I witnessed some of these encounters, but like everybody else could say nothing. If a passenger accused another with any misbehavior, other passengers would take sides and an argument could escalate to fist fights. The bus driver would ask them to stop so that he could concentrate on driving through the crowded Cairo streets. If they didn't, he would deviate from his route to the nearest police station and drop the feuding persons off to be interrogated. This would delay everybody from reaching their destination whether it was to a job, a school, or anything else. So victims suffered in silence.

One day, I felt something hard pushing against my back. The man was wearing a galabia. I knew immediately what it was. Blood boiled in my veins, but I could say nothing. As I went home, I thought of a comeback should it ever happen again. In my pocket I carried a safety pin to give the offending man a lesson by stabbing his penis with it. But I never had to use my weapon and after a few weeks I no longer carried it.

Chapter 16
MARRIAGES AND WEDDINGS

Marriage was the most important event in people's lives, especially among Christians, where there was no divorce. I do not remember a single case where a Christian marriage ended in divorce. The situation regarding divorce was different among Muslims where a man could divorce his wife by uttering three times to his wife with two male witnesses, "You are divorced."

Most marriages up to the 1940s were arranged by both families with the couple having little to say in the matter, especially the bride. In a patriarchal society a man was equal to two women. This was clear in court cases where one man or two women were needed as witnesses. Also, in inheritance, the boys got twice as much as the girls.

Marrying a cousin was the norm for centuries. This kept the land, as most people were farmers, in the family. Also, family members grew together and knew each other. Parents of both the boy and the girl knew from their observation which boy was suitable for which girl. However, marrying outside the extended family became more frequent in the twentieth century. That person, especially the man, had to have special qualities, such as being rich, well educated, or from a prominent family. Compatibility was the major reason; love was not. Over time, with fewer people employed in farming and the migration of boys to towns and cities for jobs, marriage arranged by families became less common. However, a marriage had to be approved by the parents in order to take place. Elopement or secret marriages were unheard of.

Muslim men could marry up to four women at a time. Very few did so, mainly for economic reasons. Yet, two women for one man happened occasionally. There were many reasons for it, such as the first wife not being able to produce boys or any children, or she had reached menopause, while the man wanted more children, or, occasionally, simply to enjoy sex with a younger woman.

At the universities, of course, boys met girls and some fell in love. However, dating had to be in secret, or specifically blessed by the girl's parents. Very few marriages happened during college years, mainly for economic reasons. The situation, naturally, changed when they graduated, were employed, and especially if they found jobs in a city away from their parents. However, parental approval after the usual thorough investigation of each other's families was the norm. It was rare to do otherwise. If there were major objections from either family, the newlyweds would be shunned, at least for a period. What usually brought the families back together was the birth of a grandchild.

Engagements were simple. They were customarily held in the girl's home with only the family and close friends. A religious man attended such as a priest for Christians and an imam for Muslims but their only role was to say a short prayer and bless the bride and groom-to-be. There was an exchange of rings, gold for Christians and silver for Muslims. Afterwards, food was served and pictures taken. From that time on, the couple could go out together. However, showing affection in public was an abomination. Holding hands was the most they could do. Never kissing in public. No sexual relations, either. A girl who accepted such acts would probably be shunned by her fiancé as a loose girl, who would probably cheat on him after marriage. Virginity for the girl was a must.

It might take many months for the two families to complete the preparation for the wedding, which included custom-made furniture, finding an apartment, having a wedding dress made, and other issues. Frequently, no suitable apartment could be found so newlyweds lived with one of the families for a while until they found a place of their own. It was during the months between engagement and marriage that problems often arose. If the differences were irreconcilable, the agreement was terminated and the rings and some others items returned. Being engaged and disengaged several times might put a cloud on a girl, making her future chances for marriage less likely. In a small city, rumors abounded about the reasons for the termination of an engagement, often with people taking sides. Very few minded their own business. I guess they found the stories juicy, and it filled some empty brains with entertaining gossip among the women in town. Often the damage to a reputation was greater because of those women than from the real reasons.

Engagements were not an official event, and were neither civic nor religious. Marriage, though, was very different. It was a commitment for life among Christians. Only death separated them. There was, however, an escape called an annulment, which was for very limited reasons and proclaimed only by a clerical council that took years to accomplish. A miserable life was not an acceptable reason for the church to grant a divorce.

Once the wedding date was agreed upon, several activities were put into motion. For Christians, they included reserving a church, organizing a reception with all its details, sending invitations, and the like. There was no required civic registration beforehand. The priest or imam filled out the required papers and submitted them to the Office of the Registrar for the city, which was under a national government ministry. Muslims had what is called the written or marriage agreement, usually handled in the bride's house, and was a simple document. The legal papers were always filed with the signatures of all involved including the bride and groom, both fathers, and two male witnesses.

For Coptic Christians, the wedding ceremony and the paperwork were only done in the church, and followed by the reception somewhere that very same day. The church service lasted about one hour. It included joyful hymns and reading certain chapters from the Bible. The most memorable scene however, was when the priest placed a golden robe on the groom similar to a priestly robe, and a crown on the head of both bride and groom. They looked like a king and queen. At the end of the service, the newlyweds knelt in front of the altar while the priest, or a bishop if there was one, gave them final blessings and advice for a harmonious life. Shrill cries of joy, called "zaghareet," would fill the air from women whose tongues could vibrate ten times per second.

Later, both Muslim and Christian bride and groom went to the reception. In large cities, receptions were held in hotels or special halls. In small cities and villages a large tent was erected next to the house.

There were dining tables and chairs for guests, and a large stage that rose several feet for entertainment. Almost always there were performers and belly dancers. Rich families had enormous tents and hired well known singers, dancers, and musicians from Cairo. We were delighted to hear singers who came from the capital city and whose voices we often heard on the radio. For us boys it was like going to a live theater for free. Also on the stage were the bride and groom who sat on special gold-trimmed chairs like royal thrones.

The celebration lasted many hours, usually starting after sunset and continuing until midnight or later. Only invited guests were allowed in. However, when we were small boys we hung around outside to hear the music and the singing, but mostly to watch from afar the belly dancers as they

moved their hips, bellies and breasts. When the dancers twirled around fast, their elaborate and full costumes rose up in the air. Occasionally boys would sneak in at the bottom edge of the stage to watch more closely. I remember one boy about nine years old telling us that from his vantage point he saw the belly dancer's flesh as she turned around fast and her dancing gown was way up. He swore that she was not wearing any underwear and that he saw her private parts. True or imaginary, we believed him. He belonged to the wedding party's families and thus was allowed into the tent.

Food was always plentiful, catered and full of aromas. It usually included a whole roasted lamb and several other types of meat, but never liquor because of the customs for both Muslims and Christians. However, as the celebrations were held next to the bride's or groom's house, many men would go in and out of the house with the excuse of going to the bathroom. I guess many did more than pee, as by the end of the night they were drunk!

After the reception, the bride and groom went to their new apartment or were given a private room in one of the parents' house to consummate the marriage. The length and place of the honeymoon depended on the family's financial situation. The morning after the wedding, family members and close friends came by to offer personal congratulations, and gave them envelopes of cash, the normal gift. Money was practical and certainly appreciated by the newlyweds in starting their lives together.

I left Egypt before any of my siblings were married.

Chapter 17
DEATH AND FUNERALS

The death of loved ones is never easy. In Egypt it was especially hard financially because there were no government assistance programs for the needy. If the father died, who was almost always the sole breadwinner, then the financial burden would suddenly fall on the woman, often with several small children. Heart attacks were common. They occurred frequently to men in their early fifties. For economic reasons, the usual age for men to marry was in their thirties. As a child I had witnessed many such deaths in the neighborhood. Extended families took care of the children, especially if both parents died in a short period, often from infectious diseases.

The more memorable deaths, however, for me were those of young people. The first one I was aware of was a thirteen-year-old boy who lived across the street. Like a lot of teenagers he had many fights with his parents. One day he must have felt life was not worth living. While his father was at work and his mother was nursing a baby in another room, he went to the kitchen, doused himself with kerosene, and lit a match. His screams brought his mother, the neighbors and people passing by to his rescue. He suffered third degree burns over most of his body and needed lots of plasma to replace his lost fluids. With a small blood bank in Beni Suef, a neighbor took the train to Cairo to get more plasma. By the time he was back, six hours later, the boy was dead. He had been a member of our street soccer team.

Another time a ten year old was changing a light bulb in an old house. For some reason, he was electrocuted. His heart stopped. There was no such thing as CPR in those days. The hospital was ten minutes away and the boy was pronounced dead on arrival.

A twelve-year-old mentally-disabled boy liked to climb trees near an irrigation canal that was connected to the Rive Nile. In summer the canal was deep and had a swift current. For some reason, the branch of the tree that the boy was on broke, and he fell into the water. His eleven-year-old brother jumped in to save him. Both drowned. It was one of the saddest days in our neighborhood.

It was also not uncommon for infants to have what was called severe summer diarrhea, becoming dehydrated and dying within a day. Women often died during childbirth at home from severe bleeding. Many people died from infectious diseases. There were not too many people in town over sixty years old. From an early age, we came to accept death easily.

Men usually remarried if they had young children, to have a new wife to look after them, as happened with my own father. Women, on the other hand, almost never remarried after the death of their husbands, regardless of age, and often dressed in black for the rest of their lives.

It was the rule of the health department that burial must be carried out within twenty-four hours after death. Those who died in the morning would be buried that very afternoon. Those who died in the afternoon or at night were buried the following morning. There were no funeral homes. The weather was often very hot and we had no refrigeration for the bodies. All the burial preparations were made in the deceased's home, even if he or she died in the hospital. In the heat, bodies would decompose fast and the smell of death would fill the air if left beyond twenty hours. Preparation was similar whether the deceased was Muslim or Christian. The funeral and burial rituals, however, were different.

The family of the deceased washed the body with soap and water and then wrapped it in white sheets, covering the body from the feet to the head with a handkerchief tied at the top. It was probably the same way the ancient Egyptians wrapped their dead as did the Jews at the time of Jesus. Then the undertaker came with the casket.

Muslims used a plain, simple wood casket with four handles. The body was placed inside and the casket was nailed shut. No open caskets. Very rarely would an autopsy be done because people felt it was a desecration of

99

the body. Only if a crime was suspected would there be an autopsy. Christians used a fancier casket.

With very little time between death and burial and no telephones in ninety-nine percent of the homes, the way to relate a death to relatives around the country was by telegram. The obituary section in the most circulated paper in the country would mention the death and funeral one or two days later. The friends of the deceased would send condolence telegrams. Others would send their condolences through the obituaries in the newspaper the following days. The number of telegrams received and the space in the obituaries denoted the status of the deceased and his family.

The procession for Muslims was to the nearest mosque. Family members or close friends carried the coffin on their shoulders while chanting continuously in unison saying, "There is no God but Allah, Mohammed is his Messenger."

As they entered the mosque they chanted a short prayer, and then proceeded to the River Nile. The city of Beni Suef was built on the western bank of the river. The non-fertile area, mostly desert, was on the eastern side where the cemeteries were situated. Most mourners went back to their jobs or their homes, but the family and close friends took a large sailboat to the other side of the river. By then the cemetery guard would have been informed by the family of the need for burial and for whom.

The wrapped body of the Muslim was taken out of the wooden coffin, and placed into an area that had already been dug to accommodate it, probably three or four feet deep. The body was laid to rest in it, and then soil was heaped on. The casket was taken back by the undertaker. A stone was usually placed where the head of the deceased was buried. The head was always placed to point to Mecca.

Christian funerals were somewhat different. There were usually one or two churches in small cities. The deceased was put into a fancy casket, as he would be buried in it. The casket was loaded onto a carriage pulled by two horses draped in a black blanket with large crosses on it. Deacons dressed in their formal church attire walked ahead of the carriage chanting special church hymns for the dead, while family and friends walked behind the carriage with men first and wailing women behind.

In a small city, and with a minority of Christians, almost everyone knew everyone else. Through word of mouth and from window to window or balcony to balcony, everyone learned of a death. Those who didn't would hear the mournful melodies of the deacons, and would come out to their balconies to watch the procession. They often dressed in a hurry and went to the church. Church bells rang sad tunes for about a half hour before the funeral service. People could hear it far and wide.

The Christian funeral service lasted about forty minutes. There were special hymns and readings from the Bible. After the service, the procession of the family and close friends proceeded to the river bank while most of the other people offered their condolences at the outside door of the church and went back to their regular life. The burial cemetery for Christians was separate from that of the Muslims. Christian graves were like a small bungalow. The upstairs had a kitchen and a few chairs, and the downstairs had many large shelves. The coffin of the newly-deceased person was placed on the shelves. After several years, many of the coffins were opened and all the bones put into one coffin to leave space for future burials.

The family would stay a while to rest in the living area, perhaps eating food they brought with them, and then they took the sail boat that was usually waiting for them for a few hours, back to the western bank. Those burial homes were often visited the day before each major religious holiday by the family who stayed all day, remembering the dead, and giving food or money to the multitude of beggars who flocked to those places on the designated days.

The above description applied to many villages, towns and small cities. Cairo, Alexandria and other large cities had slightly different ways due to distances and the need for multiple cemeteries around the cities, where the coffins were transported in cars. The Khalil family burial site is connected to a 1,300-year old church in old Cairo. My father was buried there in 1972. The rest of my family, however, immigrated to United States and my mother and brother were buried in Los Angeles.

The three days after a person died were a very important time for the family. There is a belief that the spirit of the deceased stays around for three days before it ascends to the heavens. Priests recite a special prayer in the home on the third day called The Release of the Soul Prayer. Perhaps the more practical reason is that many of the relatives or close friends from other towns could not make it to the funeral in time. Hence, they traveled to offer their condolences after burial, which might be a day or two later. Another significant day was the fortieth day after death. This was when a church service was carried out, perhaps to provide closure to the sad event or perhaps just an old Egyptian custom.

But the most intense mourning took place over the first three days. Relatives and friends, especially women, congregated in the house all day, while men only came after work to offer their condolences. The family served black Turkish coffee with no sugar as a sign of sadness. There were professional mourners, mostly older widows, dressed in black and well versed in chanting. These women were very good at making rhyming verses to suit the name and the situation of the deceased. They wailed between chanting, increasing the intensity of their wailing every time a new person entered the house, especially the relatives of the deceased who came from far away.

From my balcony in the morning, I could see several of these older widows, dressed in black, walking to wherever there had been a funeral the previous day. They had a lot of free time on their hands, let alone being able to drink free coffee all day as well as being served a free lunch! Neighbors and friends brought food for everyone to share, thus sparing the family of the deceased from cooking, and assuring that no one went hungry among the mourners, especially those from out of town.

For many, especially richer families, a very large tent was erected on a side street next to the house. It stretched over almost the whole width of the street, leaving only a few feet for those living on that street to access their homes. The length of the tent varied from sixty to a hundred feet. The top, about ten to twelve feet high, was made of heavy material, similar to that used for our movie theater during the winter. Large kerosene lamps hung at several points and chairs were placed in a U-shaped arrangement. There was always a small head table at the end of the tent where a Muslim imam would recite from the Koran, or a Coptic priest would read from the Bible and give a short sermon on life and death, sin and repentance, and the like. Special waiters, dressed in long white robes with red cloth wrapped around their waists, walked among the mourners serving freshly-made black coffee.

This affair usually started just after sunset for about two hours and for only one night, on the evening of the burial day, but occasionally on a different night if a lot of the mourners were expected to come from far-away towns. Almost all of the local people attended the first night only. I personally witnessed two such funerals on our small street. It was practical and served the purpose as there were no large halls in town for such occasions.

If the father died and the mother couldn't afford to raise the children, they would be sent to an orphanage. The city had two Muslim orphanages, one for boys and one for girls. Christians in town, who made up ten percent of the population, were too few to need an orphanage. Other people and the church usually supported poor families with the expenses of keeping the children at home.

Chapter 18
MY HIGH SCHOOL YEARS

In my mind, high school years open a bud into a flower, which in adult years brings forth fruit. As a bud opens, so does a teenager's body, his mind, and his social and spiritual relationships. So it was with me.

In Egypt at the time, high schools were five years, from eighth to twelfth grade. Boys and girls attended separate schools. There were three high schools in town for boys, two public and the private Coptic school which I attended till seventh grade. After that my father enrolled me in the more prestigious Prince Farouk Secondary School known for its high academic standard. It was a great school, situated at the eastern edge of town near the River Nile. The building was two stories high and U-shaped. The school was surrounded by a limestone fence six feet high and had a large metal gate manned by a sergeant in uniform.

There were thirty classrooms, six for each grade. The grounds included a soccer field, a basketball court, and a large cafeteria. The horticulture area was full of vegetables, fruits and flowers, and had a full-time gardener.

The bathroom had about ten toilets, oriental style where one had to squat to do the job, plus ten urinals, and ten sinks with cold water faucets only. On one side of the large building complex were the teaching staff offices, teachers' lounge and a large room for supplies. A separate building at the other end of the school grounds housed the chemistry lab and the art center.

School started at 8 a.m. and ended at 2:45 p.m. on Saturday, Sunday, Tuesday and Wednesday, but ended at noon on Monday (mid-week) and

Thursday. Friday was our weekend day in all government-run institutions, while Christian schools had Sundays off instead. There were six periods each full day and four periods on Monday and Thursday. The periods were fifty minutes long with five minutes between them. Recess was thirty minutes from 9:45 a.m. to 10:15 a.m. and lunch hour was from noon to 1 p.m.

Students began arriving at 7:30 a.m. The bell rang at 7:55 a.m. for students to go to class and again at 8 a.m. to start instruction. The sergeant was responsible for ringing the bell all day. After he rang the bell, he closed the metal gates. Any student who came after that had to go to the Vice-Principal's office before being permitted to go to class. He would get scolded, and if he repeated the offense of being late, he had to bring a note from his parents as to the reason for the delay. It was humiliating to be late, as he would be booed by his classmates when entering the class.

Each student had his own wooden desk, about two feet wide, with a large lockable drawer wherein books not needed for homework could be kept overnight. There was a different teacher for every subject, all men, of course, in a boys' school. Whether the class was fun or boring depended on the teacher rather than the subject. I remember fondly a geography teacher who made us almost live in the country we were studying, with stories and anecdotes and lots of imagination. His descriptions of America with its great geography, rivers and lakes, its people, industry, and monuments, were fascinating. Combined with the glamour of life in Hollywood, the teacher made us yearn to visit that far-away country. Harry Truman was the U.S. president then and was admired for his courage.

Another person was Sheikh Ahmed, the Arabic teacher. He praised me for memorizing a great deal of poetry and passages of the Koran, which we studied as Arabic literature, telling me, "Though Christian, you are better than the Muslim students." He encouraged me to write poetry and helped correct this extra-curricular activity. He made me enjoy writing. To him I owe my love for the Arabic language.On the other hand, some classes were dull, or hard, or too long. Too much material was given to us in some classes within the fifty-minute period. I was the only student in eighth grade who owned a wrist watch and was always getting tapped on my back by students behind me asking how many more minutes till the period ended. Sometimes the teacher heard the whisper and got upset. He frequently told me to stop looking at the watch or he'd take it away from me. He never did. After all, I was the star student able to answer all the questions posed by the general education inspectors who visited the schools periodically. They were sent by the Ministry of Education to check on the students' learning and the ability of the teachers to teach. Their reports would have an impact on the teacher's chance of promotion either to a head teacher of his subject with a higher salary, or to move to a larger school, or a more desirable city.

The author visiting his Beni Suef high school in the 1960s.

Subjects we studied included three languages: Arabic, English and French. Math, algebra, geometry, physics, chemistry, biology and art were taught at different grades and levels. There were no electives until the twelfth grade, when we had to choose extra classes either in humanities, the sciences, or advanced mathematics. These were prerequisites for admission to certain colleges such as the sciences for health care or general science, mathematics for engineering and business, and the humanities for colleges of art, law, and languages. Due to several teacher exchange programs, we had teachers from England and France. Their classes were very hard work as we were only allowed to communicate with them in their own language, becoming proficient in their dialect and pronunciation. However, the classes gave us a fine education in preparation for university.

There was homework every night, often in multiple subjects. It usually took from two to four hours to finish them all, including weekends. As our house was noisy with my several young siblings I often went up to our rooftop to study in peace. Here, the only disturbance was from the chickens or ducks we raised.

After dark I depended on electricity to study but there were frequent blackouts that could last for several hours. One time we were told that some field rats ate the electrical cables, another time there was an overload. At other times a fuse might blow, or replacement parts would be needed. Whatever the reason, it was irritating. Thank God for kerosene lamps. Sometimes three or four of us would sit around a table with a kerosene lamp in the center. Many a night only its faint light was all we had to do our homework, for there were no excuses for not finishing an assignment, even an illness unless we were hospitalized.

A kerosene lamp was used to study during frequent blackouts.

We went to bed between 8 p.m. and 9 p.m. during the six-day school week. My best time to study was in the early morning before school. We lived next to a mosque. When the Muezzin called for the early-morning prayer from the top of the minaret at 5 a.m., I would wake up, put some clothes on, and head out to a nearby park to study at daybreak. Many other boys in their teens did the same. It was quiet there. Our minds were fresh after a good night's sleep and thus conducive to learning. By 7 a.m. I would be back home ready to leave for school. The watch that my father bought me when I was ten made my life a lot easier as I could keep an eye on the time.

Lunch was offered at school at no cost to the students. I guess it was a government program to help with nutrition as many students came from poor families. From 1946 to 1948, we were served a hot lunch of rice, vegetables and meat for the all-day school. There were no meals on Thursdays as it was only a half-day. Our favorite was the Monday meal. Although it was also a half-day, the staff hoped that students would stay on the school grounds for the sports programs. Attendance was encouraged, but not mandatory. Many students forfeited the noon meal and went home. The cafeteria, with its pre-set food on the tables, would be half empty. After we ate we walked around collecting oranges or whatever fruits were left on the tables, filling our pockets, unless, of course, there were pieces of watermelon.

Then in 1949, for some reason, the government was not able to provide hot lunches. They were substituted by cheese sandwiches. We were told that the cheese was donated by America. The fruit, of course, was still provided locally.

I was good at sports but could not match the bigger boys who were older, taller, and stronger, so I was never picked to be on a competitive school team. I did excel in gymnastics and occasionally enjoyed performing various routines during lunch time. There were, however, no coaches as such, so one had to learn by watching and imitating the older boys. Also, I enjoyed the physical education classes given twice a week. They mostly comprised of running, muscle building and aerobic exercises. However, there was no such thing as P.E. clothing, or tennis shoes, or lockers. Many students played soccer or basketball during part of the lunch hour or for a brief time after school, but only a handful could participate from among the 900 enrollees. I usually spent my lunch time studying. I went home immediately after the last period.

Some unforgettable incidents come to mind. Our math teacher who finished a class early said that he was going to discuss with us a report written by an American called Kinsey. The report was about sex. Most of us students were thirteen to sixteen years old and we were eager to hear something scientific about the subject. However, two boys from very conservative families objected, saying that they came to school to learn math, not sex. The teacher took a vote. The majority wanted to hear about the Kinsey Report, and the two boys were excused to spend the rest of the time in the schoolyard. That class was very interesting!

One period a week was devoted to religious instruction. Students were separated by Christians and Muslims. As there were more Muslim students, they stayed in the classroom with an official Muslim sheikh for instruction from the Koran. There was no official teacher for Christians so usually a Christian teacher of any subject would take the Christian students on a voluntary basis. We'd sit under a tree, read the Bible and have a discussion. All students, however, were exposed to the Koran as part of the Arabic language instruction with no emphasis on dogma. We had to memorize excerpts from the Koran as part of Arabic literature, which was important for taking the year-end exam, but there was no test in religion as such, for either Muslims or Christians.

The Prince Farouk High School was about one mile from our house. It took about twenty minutes to walk there. Kids from neighboring houses usually walked together, chatting and joking along the way. On a few cold winter mornings we'd hire a carriage drawn by a horse from the nearby carriage post. It took five kids and we shared the fare. We felt very grand when we arrived in style at school. But we didn't do it often as it was relatively expensive and we had to use our allowances to pay for it. When the weather had warmed up a bit in the afternoon, we'd walk home. Only two or three students came by car. Their families were rich and they always had a chauffeur. It didn't bother us but I'm sure we hid some jealousy deep inside!

There was no such thing as social activities at school. Instead, there were several service clubs in town. They were mostly run by religious organizations for Muslims or Christians. However, sports activities were highly important. Each school in the province and in neighboring provinces was proud of its soccer, basketball, and volleyball teams. They were the only recognized interscholastic sports. Our soccer team was the best in the area. We won the championship for several years in a row and some of the good players went on to join professional teams in Cairo.

We were frequently given academic tests. Some were scheduled, such as the mid-year comprehensive exam in all subjects, but any teacher could give a pop quiz at any time. So we had to be prepared for the unexpected although the pop tests had no bearing on our final score of any subject. Results only counted for the end of the year exam, in June. However, low scores indicated a weakness in a specific subject. Thus, private tutoring during the final two months of the year was common. Students benefited and teachers earned extra income, including my father, who was a well-respected math teacher.

The final exams were very important. If a student failed in many subjects he had to repeat the school year. Some students who were either not too smart or didn't work hard could spend two years in each grade. This resulted, as can be imagined, in wide age discrepancies between students in any given grade. However, if the student failed in only one or two subjects, he could take a make-up exam at the end of summer. If he passed, he moved up to the next grade. If he failed, even in a single subject, he had to repeat the entire grade with all of its subjects.

The most dreaded exam was the twelfth grade National Examination. The results of that exam decided many aspects of one's life and future. The top five percent of the students could choose any college, usually medicine for science majors and engineering for math majors. Other colleges came after that. About 10,000 students took that exam the year I graduated, in June 1951. The exam lasted six days, six hours a day, from 8 a.m. to 11 a.m., and from 1 p.m. to 4 p.m. Each session was devoted to one subject and required a lot of writing. There were no multiple choice questions. We'd sit in a large hall, in rows, supervised by several teachers from another school. No one was allowed to talk, eat or drink. No questions could be asked. If a student needed to go to the bathroom, he was escorted by a teacher who waited outside the toilet and escorted him back.

June in Egypt is hot, with temperatures hovering around a hundred degrees Fahrenheit. There was no air conditioning. The tension was palpable and sweat was obvious. Some students fainted. They were taken out immediately so as not to disrupt the others. They may or may not have been allowed back, depending on their condition. Talking or cheating, if caught, was punished by a warning, and followed on the second offense by expulsion. It was a nerve wracking week. The college one attended was based on that week's results and decided a person's income for life, his social standing, and even his marriage. High class, rich, or well-educated girls wanted to marry a top-of-the-line college graduate, especially if he was in medicine.

The one-month waiting period between the exam and the announcement of the national results from Cairo was tough to bear. The examination papers from all over Egypt were taken to the Ministry of Education in the capital. The students were given numbers and their names didn't appear on the exam papers. Teachers were recruited from around the country and paid well to evaluate the thousands of anonymous papers.

Finally, the results were announced after being certified by the Minister of Education personally. They were reported on national radio by province, school, and the number of students who passed or failed in each school. No individual names were mentioned. Each school received its results by name

The author in high school.

and grade through a courier that same day and the results were posted immediately, usually the following morning at 9 a.m. Students, and sometimes their families, flocked to the school at 6 a.m. or 7 a.m. to wait for the results that would decide each person's future. As the students saw their scores, there would be laughing or crying, or simply total silence. They went home to contemplate the significance of what they saw. Students who failed one or more subjects could take a make-up exam at the end of the summer. But the twelfth-grade exam is very different from all other grades, in which if you passed you moved on to the next grade. Those who passed the twelfth-

111

grade make-up exam, regardless of their score at the end of summer, received a D or simply the minimum passing score which would obviously affect their college admission. Many such students forfeited the make-up exam and simply repeated the year, hoping for a better score next time around. Sadly, the number of teenage suicides increased dramatically during that week.

I was very pleased to have scored in the ninety-seventh percentile of the whole country and was assured a place in the King Fouad University College of Medicine, a seven-year program. The name was changed to Cairo University in 1954. I felt a little weird but proud when friends and neighbors came to our house to congratulate my dad on his doctor son. I was just fifteen years old! There was a big celebration at our house. As was our custom, visitors dropped by to share the joy and be offered a drink of sweetened mixtures of fruit juice and rose water. I was the first boy in the neighborhood to go to medical school.

That was probably the happiest summer of my teen years. My future was assured and my family was very proud. My rich uncle invited me and my younger brother to spend a week in the resort city of Alexandria, and my entire extended family treated this short fifteen-year-old kid with great respect, often calling me Dr. Elhamy.

One of the worst summers when I was in high school was in 1947. The calamity that befell Egypt was known as the cholera epidemic. It came from Saudi Arabia during the Hajj season when over a million Muslims from around the world would descend on Mecca for the annual pilgrimage. Some of the pilgrims were from countries where pockets of endemic cholera often existed, such as the new country called Pakistan. With poor sanitation and overcrowding it was easy to see how fast intestinal diseases could spread.

It was first announced that cases of cholera were discovered in an eastern province near Suez, with a number of deaths. Cholera can cause severe diarrhea with fatal dehydration and electrolyte depletion in a matter of a day or less, especially in children. The incubation period is two to three days, which makes it a fast-moving disease with a high fatality rate.

This time the epidemic was voracious, with whole families dying. Everyone was scared, and overcrowded clinics were causing panic. The treatment facilities could not possibly cope with the number of casualties.

The government mobilized its resources. The World Health Organization donated several million doses of cholera vaccine which were given as two injections, one week apart. People lined up by the thousands to get their shots.

Travel was restricted between towns by train, bus and car, unless one had an identification card with a photo and stamp from the Public Health Department and the date of immunization. Every day the radio announced the number of new cases and the number of deaths in every province and major cities. It was frightening to hear that one province had 4,000 cases that day with 250 deaths, etc. All the statistics were published in the national daily newspapers. One could follow the trend of where it was spreading and later, the decline in the number of cases and deaths.

Precautions were announced: water had to be boiled before drinking. All fruits and vegetables that were normally eaten raw had to be soaked in potassium permanganate before eating, which tasted awful but the alternative was possible death.

School openings were postponed for a few weeks, until the epidemic began to wane and almost all of the population was vaccinated. One could only enter the school grounds after passing a security gate showing his cholera vaccination I.D.

The immediate and severe restriction on people's travel, the scare in people's minds as far as food was concerned, and the help of the W.H.O., drastically decreased the spread of the disease which could have been as bad as the plague in Europe in the 1300s because of the lack of running water in many small towns, or indoor latrines. One could see that most cholera cases were in the north, with the number of dead decreasing from each province in a southerly trend.

Within a couple of months, life returned to normal but with tens, probably hundreds of thousands, dead from the cholera epidemic of 1947.

Chapter 19
MY MEDICAL SCHOOL YEARS

I was fortunate to have had a great primary and secondary education that prepared me for life, especially my years at medical school. It was not only about learning the practice of medicine. We also learned how to deal with people of all ages and at all levels of society.

The educational system in Egypt was modeled after the British system of almost-continuous six and a half calendar years. There were no Christmas vacations and only three summers off during the whole program. There was no goofing off or short cuts. I had many sleepless nights, occasional feelings of despair that I would ever make it, and endless studies and assignments. Yes, the rewards were great but the road was hard.

My medical training began in August 1951. I received a notice that I was accepted by the King Fouad College of Medicine. It didn't come as a surprise to me as my ranking was No. 104 among the 4,000 students in the science section who took the national high school exam, called the Secondary Schools Baccalaureate Exam. King Fouad University admitted 400 students to Medical School every year. About 100 of them dropped out by the end of the first year, with a few dropouts every succeeding year. Approximately 250 usually graduated.

There were no student interviews for several reasons, one being the huge number of applicants, and another was that many professors had different standards or were not objective. More important, though, was the possibility of discrimination. This could be based on religion, on how one dressed, spoke, or whether he came from a prominent family. Bribes in Egypt in different forms were not unheard of at any level. Thus, the final score in the Secondary School final exam was the fairest metric for admission.

There were three medical schools in Egypt: two in Cairo and one in Alexandria. These public universities charged moderate tuition. It would have been difficult for my father to pay tuition for his nine children to attend college, even though, of course, we did not all attend at the same time. Fortunately, there was a law that exempted children of teachers from having to pay for tuition. So our only expenses were for books and other regular charges. Rent, though, was high in Cairo, especially near the universities. Luckily, my father kept one apartment in his six-apartment building unrented. It was also not too far from the medical school which meant that I could walk, thus avoiding the erratic transportation system in Cairo. The first year studies, however, were held at the major campus in Giza where we took classes with the Science Major students. Also, my sister, who was one year behind me, had been accepted at a prestigious high school for girls in Cairo so we would both live in the apartment.

My sister Laila and I left Beni Suef together in September 1951. She was a good cook and, of course, we kept each other company. My father took us to the bus station with two large suitcases, paid for the tickets, and bade us farewell. Laila was two years older than me but there were two reasons I was ahead of her in school. First, I entered school at a younger age and skipped second grade. Also, high school for girls was six years, while for boys it was five years. It was not that girls were considered less intelligent or industrious than boys. Girls had to study many more subjects than boys to prepare for motherhood and running a household. They studied home economics, cooking, cake making, baking, embroidery, sewing, infant care and probably other subjects. Both boys' and girls' schools had the same number of class periods every day but in order to accommodate those extra subjects for girls the academic subjects were divided into five years for boys and six years for girls.

My own first year was very hard. We studied chemistry, physics and biology in high school in Arabic. However, at the university, the classes were in English and we had to learn all the technical names and symbols in that language. In high school we had required books to study. At university there were not only the required books but also extra reading. Many of the professors and most of the department heads, until World War II, were British. Our British-trained Egyptian professors were therefore highly educated. They were very knowledgeable and their lectures were more informative than the books.

We had to continuously write as they lectured, taking voluminous notes every day. Each student had to devise a shorthand for many commonly used words only understood by him. We also had to write quickly, scribbling in a way that probably no one else could read. Perhaps that is why doctors' writing is not easy to decipher. We often missed words or sentences in our haste to get it all down, or maybe our hands simply got tired, or, God forbid, the ink in our fountain pens ran out. Several students would sit together between lectures, or at the end of the day, to compare notes and fill each other in on what was missing. The professors used a microphone in the 400-seat halls. Occasionally, the microphone didn't work and only the students in the front could hear. Many of us rushed to the front seats long before the lecture began to assure ourselves of the ability to take good notes.

The campus was huge, several hundred acres, with a lot of buildings and around 15,000 students attending the various colleges. At any given time, students would be walking and talking outside. Since all the lecture halls had to keep the windows open as there was no air conditioning, there was a certain amount of noise at all times. Some lectures were boring either because of the subject or the professor's style of teaching. Students who were not really eager to learn sat in the back chatting with one another or with the girls next to them. For some boys, it was the first time in nine years for them to sit next to a girl. Most of the students were in their late teens.

Some of the girls complained to the professors of distraction and low-key harassment. Thus, the first row in each lecture hall was reserved for girls only. Maybe some of the older, or not so old, professors preferred to see pretty teen girls in front of them. Some of the back benches often made so much noise that the professor had to stop the lecture and, on a few occasions, dismiss the offenders from the class. The professors normally closed the doors as they entered which meant that late-comers were out of luck, to the detriment of their education.

About ninety percent of the students and ninety-five percent of the professors were male. Most of the female faculty held ranks either as an instructor, lecturer or assistant professor. I don't remember any female full professor or head of a department. In high school we stayed in the same classroom while teachers moved between classes. At university, it was the opposite. We went to different lecture halls for different subjects, rushing from one hall to another to assure good seats. The first lecture, usually at 8 a.m., was the worst. Most students came from all over Cairo, which had 2 million inhabitants at the time.

I took two trams from our house to the College of Science campus. They were erratic, to say the least. One could wait for half an hour at the tram stop and when it did arrive it was crowded. There were no actual doors to close and people simply stood on the steps, holding on. During rush hour passengers were stacked like sardines. The tram waited very briefly at each stop. If we weren't close enough to the exit we probably didn't have enough time to get off. People often hopped on or off while the tram was slowing down or starting to move. It was quite a skill to do so without injury.

Once I almost missed my tram ride and could have injured myself badly. In order not to be late for a lecture, I jumped on the tram as it began to move. My foot slipped. I was dragged a few feet until, thankfully, someone pulled me up, although they were cursing me. Another person said rudely, "Boy, if you want to commit suicide, do it elsewhere, or you will make us all late for work."

Needless to say, I never tried it again.

School hours were different for me, a college student with a varying schedule, while Laila in twelfth grade had set hours at school. Some days, when I came home early, I'd go out to the nearby market and buy meat, vegetables and fruit, and start cooking. Other days she would cook. Learning in the kitchen with my mother came in handy. We usually cooked stew, with meat and vegetables, making enough for the two days it would last without spoiling. This way we wouldn't waste time cooking every day. Occasionally we opened cans of sardines or fava beans and cooked the fava beans mixed with scrambled eggs.

Our custom was to store some foods in earthenware containers. Our stored foods included lentils, fava beans, rice, honey, feta cheese, cooked butter, and dried vegetables. They were important as we occasionally ran out of money for food near the end of the month. We had to depend on the income from the renters of the other apartments in our father's building. Sometimes they were late or claimed that they had no money that month for some reason. My father came periodically for a day, assured himself that our supplies were adequate, and then visited with his sisters nearby. His occasional visits helped in collecting the rent so we had money for food.

117

Our apartment had four bedrooms, a living room, a dining room, one bathroom and a kitchen/shower combination. The apartment house was built in the nineteenth century when people normally took a shower or bath only once a week, so it was considered to be a waste of useable space to have an area just for the shower. Moreover, there was no heating system, so it was cold water showers only. Water was heated in the kitchen during the winter, where we also took baths. This was different from our more modern house in Beni Suef which was built in the early twentieth century with a separate bath. At the Cairo apartment my sister and I had a bedroom each. The third bedroom was used for food storage, and the fourth bedroom was for my dad when he visited.

That first year was difficult but manageable. I spent my time studying and keeping house on weekdays. Weekends, however, were spent on church activities. As soon as the final examinations were finished, Laila and I spent that summer in Beni Suef. A month later I was relieved to learn that I passed all my subjects with good grades. I was then headed for the University Hospital for the remainder of my medical school years. This was welcome as it was a twenty-minute walk from our residence, saving me time, money, energy and the headaches of public transportation.

The most important political news during my first university year was the upheaval in government. There was turmoil in Iran. A prime minister there nationalized the oil industry against the will of the Shah of Iran. Shortly thereafter, the shah dismissed the government and another prime minister was installed by the king, but was soon assassinated. There was upheaval among the university students against all kings, Farouk of Egypt included.

The King of Egypt dismissed the democratically elected government. He appointed a new government but it lost parliamentary confidence votes and was replaced by another which suffered the same fate. There was chaos in Cairo. On January 26th, 1952, a large student demonstration from the two universities in Cairo and many high school students flooded downtown, burning cars and buses, and chanting against the king. I saw buildings on fire. A state of emergency was declared and the army descended on the city. Public transportation was halted in Cairo and all universities and schools were closed.

I wanted to go home to Beni Suef as there was no sense staying in Cairo, not knowing how long the university would be closed. There were no trams or buses to take me to the bus depot in Giza where I would take long distance buses to other cities. Since Giza wasn't affected by the demonstrations I found a donkey-pulled wooden cart and begged the man to take me there with my suitcase. Thankfully we agreed on the price and I was soon with my family, to my great relief. Cairo was scary. Many of the agitators were from the Muslim Brotherhood who disliked any civil government and wanted to establish an Islamic state, governed by the Sharia which was the law of Islamic caliphates from the seventh century till the Ottoman Empire years.

They also accused the king and his government of mishandling the war with Israel which resulted in the defeat of the Arabs. There was a rumor that the Muslim Brotherhood was going to plant explosives in all of the Christian churches simultaneously at the midnight Christmas services (Coptic Orthodox Nativity Feast is January 7th). Apparently, information about the plan was leaked to the Egyptian Secret Service and was foiled. Another major incident was the burning of a church in Suez and dragging a priest and a custodian of the church onto the street. The custodian died of his injuries but the priest survived. Christians were alarmed at this new level of violence against them by Muslim fanatics.

Universities were closed for about a month. When we returned to classes we had to make up for lost time. It was a tough year followed by a turbulent summer in which a revolution by the Army deposed King Farouk.

My next two years were devoted to basic sciences in medicine. Anatomy and physiology were studied in great detail. We dissected every part of the human body. We had no shortage of bodies as there were a lot of unclaimed corpses in Cairo from accidents and fatal diseases.

Tens of thousands of people began to move from all over Egypt to the capital, where they knew they could get jobs. Many went from place to place seeking work and their families often lost touch with them. Bodies had to be buried within twenty-four hours. However, the morgue at the University Hospital kept them a little longer in case someone claimed them. On the other hand, it had limited capacity for cadavers. Whoever was not claimed was injected with formalin and thus was ready for the anatomy classes.

Eight students would sit or stand around a body with scalpels in their hands and a book on the table. We learned every inch, every nerve and every tissue of the bodies in great detail. There were at least thirty bodies being dissected at any given time. If a certain abnormal organ or tissue was found by a group, they would invite the whole class to see it and compare. We saw many cancers and genetic defects in many organs. It gave us a great understanding of the human body and its variation in anatomy.

Many of us went even further. We bought parts of dead bodies. The morgue custodian sold them for a reasonable price. One could buy an arm, a leg, a liver, or a brain to take home for dissection and further learning. Several students would participate in buying and studying corpses. Our house was a favorite spot for this activity since we had an extra room, there were no children or pets, and my sister was not afraid to see a part of a dead body. Although the smell of formalin was terribly strong, it only took a few days to dissect an organ and the ventilation was good when all the windows were left open. No neighbors complained of the smell. These home study sessions not only helped us in the study of anatomy, but also forged strong friendships with other students which lasted many years.

The author (third from right) with his anatomy group in front of the medical school, September 1953.

Anatomy classes were not for the faint at heart. Several students dropped out. Most of us, however, got used to being around dead bodies. After the first few days we got used to the smell of formalin, too, and often stayed continuously for hours in a single session, even eating sandwiches at the table so that time was not wasted by going out for lunch.

Physiology classes were very good, even entertaining, and the professors were great. Before we learned to perform an electrocardiogram on patients we had to practice on frogs. We often bought frogs for a very reasonable price at the gate. We could buy several frogs to practice on, put them in a small bag and carry it in our pocket till we got home. One day I was riding a bus with frogs in my trouser pocket. The bus was crowded with people crushed against one another. Somehow, a frog escaped from my pocket. I heard kids screaming as they saw a jumping frog under their feet. A woman cursed whoever carried frogs on a bus but I kept my cool with a sphinxlike face. I patted my pocket, and there were still a few frogs left. I had only lost a few pennies and one frog.

Medical books were expensive. I could only afford one textbook for each subject, and sometimes a secondhand book. Most were larger than the entire Bible. For further study, we had to go and read in the library. It only had a few books for each subject and they weren't allowed to be checked out in order to be available to all the students. Between the lectures, the library, and long hours of study at home, there was very little time to rest or party.

The final exam for the basic human sciences was grueling. The written exams were comprehensive but the really difficult hurdle was the oral examination. There were two medical schools in Cairo at that time. The examiner for each school was a professor from the other school. They were tough. I guess they wanted to show that students from the rival school were not prepared. They were intimidating, putting us down if the answer didn't satisfy them. Sometimes the examiners were just plain insulting. One such examiner asked me, "How can you be trusted as a respectable physician wearing that ugly tie?"

I guess they were testing our responses and reaction under duress but it seemed like an absurd question to me. Students came out of the oral exam sweating and shaken while some girls were crying. None of the Christian girls wore a cross during the oral exams, so that they wouldn't be intimidated more than usual by a fanatic Muslim professor. Also, Christian-sounding names like George, Peter, or Mary were a dead giveaway. Most of the Muslim professors were moderate, but some were fanatic against those they considered infidels, giving Christians and Jews a hard time.

Despite my anxiety, I made it. Finally, after two continuous years in school with no summer vacation, I had a free summer. It was also the end of my sister and I being the only occupants of the apartment. The following school year my younger brother and sister were admitted to Cairo University, College of Engineering, and thus there were four of us in college at the same time. Only two of my siblings were left at home, and they were in high school. My mother shuttled between Cairo and Beni Suef to take care of the two dwellings while my father remained at home because of his job.

The following year's subjects were pathology of diseases, bacteriology, biochemistry, and pharmacology. We probably spent more hours in the labs than in the lecture halls. There was an extensive pathology museum where we could look at every conceivable disease in any organ of the body in a formalin jar. There were also thousands of slides of how diseased organs appeared under the microscope, bringing to life the saying, "a picture is worth a thousand words." It was amazing to see twenty jars of cancerous breasts at different stages and different types of cancer. This museum was superb preparation for students who wanted to study surgery and an excellent educational tool for the visualization of what various diseases can do in healthy tissue. We spent hours and hours looking through the microscopes, often having to wait our turn as there were fewer microscopes than students.

The author, far right, with other medical students and a professor in October 1956.

Pharmacology was overwhelming. We had to memorize every drug, its uses and the multitudes of side effects. We learned that there was no perfect drug and the doctor had to weigh the benefit and drawbacks of every drug for every patient. One of my friends had an uncle who was a pharmacist. We'd visit him when he wasn't busy and ask him about different drugs and the most common side effect for each. He was kind enough to show us various bottles of drugs and tell us what he usually told the customers, and what to watch for, in simple language. Those sessions gave us a deeper understanding of pharmacology than the books or the lectures.

Another successful year passed for me. President Nasser in his socialized program took over private schools among other anti-capitalist reforms, including my father's school. Government retirement age was sixty. My father was forced to retire as he became a government employee. I guess he must have been saddened by suddenly having no job, but heartened that his children received good and free college education because of his profession as a teacher.

My whole family moved to Cairo in 1956. My youngest sister and brother enrolled in high school in the neighborhood. Our house, or rather, the apartment, was crowded. Three bedrooms for eight people age from twelve to sixty! The fourth room was the guest room with a carpet and nice antique furniture. Quite often I had to study well past midnight. In order not to disturb my two brothers by having the light on while they were asleep, I often took a sleeping bag and a pillow to the guest room and studied as late as I wanted, and finally slept on the floor till morning. It was not as comfortable as sleeping on a bed but I got used to it.

The following thirty months were one long continuous term with no summer or winter vacations. There were about twenty subjects to study, both in lectures, outpatient clinics, and hospitals, for various specialties. We spent six months in general medicine and six months in general surgery, while other fields, from skin diseases to ophthalmology to gynecology and other subjects, required less time. It was grueling, to say the least.

While the lectures consumed much less time than in previous years we were on our own for the clinics. Cairo University Hospital was probably one of the largest in the world with 3,000 beds and over fifty clinics for various specialties. We had a list of them, their times and locations and it was up to us to attend as many clinics as time permitted. There were two large buildings on opposite sides of a branch of the River Nile, so I had to cross a bridge to get from one to the other. The larger hospital was a challenge to navigate and its main hallway was about a quarter mile long, providing good exercise while walking from one place to another.

As the largest hospital in the country with the most prestigious program and famous professors, patients with rare diseases from all over the country were referred to it. We saw almost every disease described in the books. There would be thirty or more cases of different rashes in one dermatology clinic, or twenty new cancer breasts in the Breast Cancer Clinic held every week. It was a great learning experience.

The inpatient experience was great too. We'd be given a lecture about a specific organ and its various diseases and told to go around the hospital and examine as many cases as we could from what we learned. For example, if we were studying the heart, we would visit the cardiac ward where there were forty beds and look at the patients' charts to find out what condition they had. We then chose some patients to interview, and examine.

The author, far left, with other medical students examining a patient.

Another learning example was a lecture about the rectum and its various diseases from hemorrhoids to cancer. We would descend on the ward where many such patients were waiting for surgery and do the same. The patients were unable to refuse because it was a teaching hospital, with no charge, and patients were being treated by the best physicians and surgeons in the country. However, many patients didn't enjoy having ten students doing a rectal exam on them in one day. Although they were not allowed to deny us, they could be belligerent and tell us the wrong symptoms.

We quickly learned to give them a little money, especially to those patients with rare diseases, and asked them to be honest with us as far as symptoms went, and permit us to do a comprehensive examination. They used the money to enjoy the luxuries that these poor patients from the countryside could not afford, such as buying cigarettes or chocolate, or to give the money to their families when they visited. Naturally, wealthy patients went to private hospitals and thus were not subjected to medical students in a public hospital.

One of the worst rotations was obstetrics. We had to observe five normal deliveries and ten complicated deliveries. Babies know nothing of schedules, of course, as in general surgery, so we were forced to hang around the obstetrics ward during non-lecture hours. When a case went to the delivery room we rushed there, day or night, hoping for a complication to satisfy our educational needs. Sometimes we sat all night with no luck. The complications had to be of different categories, so one had to be at the right place at the right time. With little sleep, the following day would be very tiring.

Some incidents are hard to forget. During our psychiatry rotation we had to spend a day at a psychiatric hospital outside of Cairo. The professor and the students took a chartered bus to the huge facility, with many buildings on thirty acres. On the grounds we saw a man standing on a bench shouting profanities against President Nasser. We were shocked as no one would dare to insult a ruler in the Middle East, be it a king or a president. There were strict laws against insulting the authorities and many would end up in jail. We thought that someone should stop the man but the professor indicated that he wouldn't be tried or convicted because he was insane. I wondered if he was really insane and had to be confined to a psychiatric hospital, or if he did say the same thing prior to his admission, which was the reason for his commitment. To me it was totalitarian rule at its worst. I think that he probably spent the rest of his life there.

Another patient was about to be released and was asked by the professor about what he would do after years of incarceration in a mental hospital. He unabashedly said that he had no skills, but could make a living by offering a room in his apartment for sex. On further inquiry, he said he would advertise renting a room by the day for anyone of either gender to do whatever they wanted at a price. There were no motels for such activities in Egypt at that time. I guess he was an off-beat entrepreneur. His treating physician said that the man's release would be denied on the grounds that he was still hallucinating. Unfortunately, there were no effective psychiatric drugs at that time.

The final exams were held in June and December of every year and lasted about three weeks each. The class was divided into two groups, one for medicine and all medical specialties, the other for general surgery and all surgical specialties. Written and oral tests were similar to what we'd gone through in previous years: tough tests, intimidating examiners, and many sleepless nights. Our final clinical exam, however, also included live patients in every field. A student was taken to a room with one patient, given a half or one hour, depending on the subject, and asked to reach a diagnosis and plan of action. This was a test of knowledge but also a matter of luck and diplomacy. Some of the patients had rare diseases and used as specimens for many exams. It would be a stroke of luck if that patient was examined by us during our studies the previous year.

When we bribed patients, they were expected to cooperate and give us an honest history. And if he liked one of us, he might even reveal his diagnosis. In some cases there was a communication barrier. We studied medicine in English but the patients spoke only Arabic, and often with a very different dialect, especially from the southern part of Egypt. When the hour was over, the professor would walk in, ask us to present the case, and show him how we reached our conclusions. Occasionally, he would ask us to show the clinical findings on the patient. Annoyingly, the professors never told us if we did well or not.

The month between the end of the final exam and the results was a time of relief that it was over, but we were, of course, very anxious about our results. The final score in each subject could decide at what type of hospital we'd be accepted for an internship and later for a specialty training residency. My final exam was held in December 1957 and the results were announced in January 1958.

Finally, nineteen years of education were over. Now I could truly be called Dr. Elhamy! There was great jubilation in my house. My family proudly advertised my success in the social column in the largest newspaper in Cairo. My uncles, aunts, cousins and many relatives came to congratulate me and my parents as the first doctor in the Khalil family. A long chapter in the book of my life ended.

A young man from Beni Suef had become a physician at the age of twenty-two!

Chapter 20
A STUDENT HERO

There was no such thing as health insurance in Egypt in the 1950s. Those who could pay went to private doctors and usually settled the bill in cash. However, in the countryside many peasants had no cash. They often bartered with the doctor with something they raised, such as a duck, a bushel of grain, fruit, or whatever they had at the time. Those who couldn't afford a private doctor usually went to government hospitals, which were not known for good care. They were always crowded, lacked equipment and adequate supplies, and were not always sanitary. Poor people went to those hospitals only for an acute illness, a laceration, a broken bone, or were near the end of life. There was often joy in the neighborhood when a patient came home cured but naturally, the mortality rate was high.

Our house in Cairo, when I attended medical school, was in an old section of the city, inherited from previous generations. When I started my clinical years at the University Hospital, our neighbors considered me a student doctor and periodically would ask my opinion about some illnesses before they went to a doctor or a hospital. After all, my opinion was free and I was one of the good neighborhood boys.

My first case was a seven-year old boy whose family thought he had tonsillitis but was not improving. They lived a few houses down from ours. I was asked by his father to see him. When I asked the boy to say the usual "aah" while depressing his tongue with the handle of a metal spoon as the father shone a flash light into his son's mouth, I saw a thick gray membrane. It looked like diphtheria. With a narrow throat the boy's breathing was laborious. I told the family what I thought and that they should take him to the hospital.

The father asked, "What will they do there?"

"The boy needs medicine immediately," I said.

"Let's go to the nearest pharmacy," he replied.

In those days we didn't need a prescription to buy most medicines. We only had to describe the symptoms to the pharmacist and he'd sell us the medication and explain how to administer it. We did just that. The pharmacist agreed with my diagnosis. Within two days the boy was cured and I was considered a hero! My reputation as a clinician spread around the neighborhood even though I still had two years to graduate from medical school.

Another boy had a fever for a week. In Egypt at that time, any fever over three days was considered typhoid until proven otherwise. An old doctor prescribed medication for it. The fever didn't go away after three days. The family called me for a second opinion. The boy's fever was very high but occurred only every other day. That was the cardinal sign for malaria. I told them what I thought. However, medicine for malaria required a licensed doctor's prescription. I went to an intern from our church and asked him for a prescription after telling him my diagnosis. He didn't hesitate to write it out. I bought the medication and the child was started on it the same night. In four days his fever was totally gone but he was obviously anemic and his face looked pale. I told the family to buy iron pills and to give them to him for a couple of months to build up his blood. The boy was back to school in a week.

At midnight another neighbor knocked on our door and asked me to see his daughter who had severe abdominal pain. I went down with him and entered the girl's room. She was about fifteen and I was nineteen. She refused to take her clothes off to be examined. She said she had "the period."

I got mad. In a stern voice I said, "Do you want me to examine you or go to the hospital for possible surgery?"

Her father was upset with her and left the room angry. The mother calmed the girl down and helped her to remove her underwear. I half closed my eyes as I examined her abdomen to show that I was interested in her sickness and not her body. She had the typical signs for acute appendicitis. Her parents rushed her to the hospital at about 2 a.m.

129

After the operation the surgeon told the family, "I am glad you didn't wait until morning to bring her in, as her appendix was about to rupture."

My reputation soared.

Another night a hysterical middle-aged woman asked me to come immediately to see her husband who was unconscious and was snoring. She couldn't wake him up. He was in his early sixties. My examination of his eyes showed very constricted pupils, a sign of basal brain hemorrhage, which was always fatal. I asked the woman to get a doctor immediately. In half an hour a doctor arrived. Now the pupils were widely dilated and non-reactive to light. Before the doctor could finish his examination, the old man gave out his last breath. The doctor signed the death certificate and left. The woman started wailing. I was sad but there was nothing anyone could do.

Then there was a boy with leukemia who required a pint of blood every few weeks for his anemia. His treating doctor suggested that he should go to the hospital's outpatient clinic for the blood transfusions. The family asked if this could be done at home to spare them transportation, which meant a taxicab both ways with its added expense, and the often long wait at the hospital. He agreed to their suggestion if they could find somebody to give the blood and watch the vital signs. The family asked me if I could do it. I agreed. They made sure one evening every few weeks that I was home. I went to the blood bank and got the blood type as per the doctor's orders. I'd hang the blood bottle, insert the needle in the boy's vein and sit by him for about an hour making small talk and trying to cheer him up. However, within a few months the boy died. Nevertheless, the family was grateful to me.

One day a girl was beaten up by her father. She cried incessantly for a long time. Suddenly, she went into a special type of seizure. Her wrists were bent and her fingers clamped together rigidly. The family summoned me to help. She was breathing heavily, fast and deep. It was a typical case of hypocalcemia. With this kind of breathing, the carbon dioxide in the blood decreases sharply, the acidity decreases, and ionized calcium in the circulating blood goes down, leading to this type of seizure. The treatment was simple. I asked them to bring a brown paper bag and put it on her mouth immediately. The parents held her down, paper bag and all. As she breathed from the paper bag, the carbon dioxide increased in the air going to her lungs.

We could see the fingers loosen up and the wrists return to their neutral position. The shaking stopped and so did the crying. It was like a miracle. I immediately left the house as I didn't want to hear what was to follow. Child abuse was not a term used in those days.

"Thank you doctor," was all I got and was all I needed.

There must have been other stories of others I was able to help, but these are the incidents that are still vivid in my mind more than half a century later.

Chapter 21
MY INTERNSHIP IN CAIRO

An intern at Cairo University Hospital was like being a slave doctor. The work was strenuous but the rewards of the great training we received tipped the scale. In January 1958, the results of the final exam were announced, and I passed. About seventy-five percent of the students passed the first time around. The exams were held once every six months. Another twenty percent passed the second time. However, about five percent took much longer and a few never graduated. I know two such students who gave up after ten years in Medical School. One had a nervous breakdown and was admitted to a psychiatric hospital for treatment of suicidal tendencies, and the other had a major personal and family calamity.

Out of the 200 graduating students that year, the top hundred were accepted for a rotating internship year at the prestigious University Hospital, while the rest were assigned to government hospitals in Cairo and other cities. The internship program started March 1st. That meant I had the whole month of February to rest and relax from seven years of grueling study, continuous tension and sleepless nights. It was so good to sleep until eight or nine o'clock in the morning while my brothers and sisters went off to school. As there was no television in Egypt then I spent my time reading non-medical books and visiting friends and museums. It was a God-given month.

During our twelve-month program, we had to spend three months in internal medicine and three months in general surgery. The other six months were divided into sections of a few weeks each in various departments by competitive requests. Each applicant stated his or her top requests. The top-ranking students got first pick. I was in the middle of the graduating class, so I didn't get all I wanted, especially in pediatrics, as I was hoping to specialize in that branch. I specifically didn't apply for obstetrics and gynecology because of my short fingers, which would be a hindrance to conducting a proper pelvic examination.

To become a specialist in any field one had to spend several years in a residency training program at a prestigious hospital. These resident physicians were picked from top students who did well in that field during their internship year. Also, religion was a factor. Some heads of departments were fanatical Muslims and never accepted any Christian interns, regardless of their rank. This was especially obvious in ob/gyn. Many Muslim men didn't want the private parts of their wives to be seen by an infidel. Personal connections were also involved. A young doctor from a prominent political family would take precedence over others in lucrative specialty training such a neurosurgery, urology and orthopedics.

The interns' quarters were in a separate building from the hospital. The rooms were spacious and furnished with three single beds, a desk and a lamp. There was also a telephone. Interns were on call every third night. If two were on call the same night, we wouldn't know for whom the call was but it got sorted out. The bathrooms and showers were down the hall and there was a large dining room and a kitchen. The food was better than the hospital food, but no match for home-cooked food. Many interns stayed in their quarters all the time. It was their home. However, my parents' house was only twenty minutes walking distance so I went home most nights.

Interns often ate in a nearby restaurant at the beginning of the month. Our monthly stipend was the equivalent of $40, which was the average salary for a new university graduate. They often bought beer, wine and take-out shish-kabob (grilled beef with onion, tomato and green pepper on a stick) in the early days of the month but by mid-month most of the money was gone and the belt had to be tightened.

I was in a different situation. I gave my father one quarter of my salary to pay for housing for my younger sister who was studying pharmacy at the University of Alexandria, 130 miles away. She was living in the university dormitory for girls, with added costs. I saved part of the remaining salary, spending a little on entertainment or taking my family on a day trip during a weekend when I was not on call.

After a grueling seven years in medical school with nightly study often until midnight, now, having two free evenings every three days, was a luxury I wasn't used to. I decided to enroll in the night program at the Coptic Orthodox Seminary in Cairo. I didn't know what I would do with my life as a physician. One of the ideas was to be a medical missionary in Africa, thus the Seminary training might be helpful. I went one or two evenings a week depending on my work nights. Private practice in Cairo was almost impossible for young graduates as there were hundreds of well-known specialists and professors from the two medical schools. Practicing in remote villages was not appealing unless one was ordered by the government as part of the National Service.

My first rotation was in the Internal Medicine Department. Each morning the resident physician in charge of the ward of forty patients made rounds, and twice a week the staff faculty did so. The interns tagged along with notebook in hand. New admissions from the previous twenty-four hours were discussed as to diagnosis, laboratory work, and treatment. The interns took notes. For other cases the changes or progress of their condition was evaluated while the interns took notes. The rounds usually lasted one to two hours. Afterward, the interns wrote progress notes on the patients' charts and ordered the laboratory tests and new treatment as suggested from the notes they had written.

I also did brief physical examinations for some patients. It would take several hours and had to be finished by noon to be able to attend the outpatient clinic in the afternoon. This was more interesting as the intern had to participate in making the diagnosis and suggested treatment. Being a tertiary hospital we frequently saw many very rare conditions, which a practicing physician downtown may only see once a year, if that. It was excellent training.

If we didn't finish our ward work in the morning, we'd go back to do it after the outpatient clinic ended around 4 p.m. During night calls, the intern was alone, responding to patients' changing conditions and new admissions. However, a resident physician was always available if needed for advice.

The first patient to die on my watch was a devastating experience. She was a woman in her forties who was admitted for pneumonia. She also had terminal cancer. It was 11:30 p.m. After examining her I decided that she needed the new and strong antibiotic terramycin. I contacted the resident physician for his opinion. He told me we could start it in the morning as the pharmacy closed at midnight. I told him that she needed it immediately because of her grave condition and that I was willing to buy it myself from a nearby twenty-four-hour private pharmacy. He laughed and told me that I was naive.

"Since she has terminal cancer, her pneumonia is a blessing and she'll be spared weeks or months of severe pain," he said. "If her pneumonia is that bad, she'll die anyway, with or without an antibiotic."

I was disheartened but complied. Three hours later the ward nurse phoned me to come quickly as the patient was dying. By the time I got to the ward the woman had stopped breathing. Her teenaged children were around her bed with the curtain drawn, crying. I examined her and heard no heart sound and no breathing sounds. I pronounced her dead. The family's crying escalated. They bent to kiss her. I was moved and felt tears on my cheeks. Not to embarrass myself, I withdrew to the nurses' station to write notes on her chart and to sign the death certificate. Needless to say, I didn't sleep that night. I was exhausted physically and emotionally. From that day on I tried to separate my emotions from my professional duty.

Many diabetic patients were admitted to adjust the type, dose, and time for their insulin shots which was the only treatment available. This was usually done by checking their blood sugar many times a day. There was no micro testing through finger pricks. We had to get blood from the veins. Many diabetic patients were obese which made finding a vein a difficult task for the intern and a painful experience for the patient. After a while, though, I became an expert phlebotomist, using my sensitive fingers to spot a deep vein under the skin and fat.

The most difficult patients to treat were those with heart failure. The only effective medicine at that time was digitalis. However, its therapeutic range was narrow. If the patient received too little it might do no good. If too much, it might disturb the heart rhythm and perhaps lead to death. Moreover, the same dose could be right for one patient but not for another. We didn't have an easy test to measure the level of the medicine in the blood. I am almost sure that some patients died who could have been saved today. Also, there was no piped-in oxygen. We had to drag large cylinders next to the bed and connect a tube to a mask on the patient's face. The nurse had to see what level of oxygen was in the cylinder as it may not last all night and the patient could die from lack of oxygen in his blood. Also, a lighted cigarette and leaky tubing could lead to disaster. Many patients smoked in bed. Cigarettes were smuggled in by their family or friends when the nurses were not around, hiding them under the patients' pillows. The "No Smoking" signs were routinely ignored. Luckily, there were no fires that I could remember that year.

Another sad condition was water in the abdomen (ascitis) due to liver cirrhosis from the worm Bilharzia which affected at least ten percent of the peasants in the countryside. They walked barefooted in the infested water in the fields and small irrigating canals. We would sit the sufferer up, insert a large needle into his abdomen and drain a gallon of fluid into a bucket. This made breathing easier. However, within one or two weeks the abdomen got filled again which necessitated a repeat of the painful procedure.

My next rotation was the emergency room. Every night there were lacerations to suture, abscesses to drain, and sick children with infections, seizures or dehydration. During the hot weather we would have at least one scorpion bite every night. Scorpions came down from the hills just at the edge of Cairo to nearby run-down houses. Again, since most of those residents walked without shoes, most scorpion bites were on the feet. This was fortunate for the patients as it took time for the poison to rise into the rest of the body. We had anti-scorpion serum ready all the time so it was a relatively easy fix if the patient came in right away. If a condition couldn't be handled in the emergency room, such as severe bleeding or a heart attack or stroke, the patient was immediately admitted for appropriate care.

Some incidents are hard to forget. One such situation was a young man with a dislocated left shoulder. His arm was hanging down and he was obviously in pain. I had never seen such a condition before in medical school. However, I'd learned from the books how to maneuver the arm in a methodical way to bring the head of the shoulder bone back to the socket. The patient was muscular and bigger than me. I weighed only a 120 pounds and my arms were not that strong. I remembered a technique for such cases. It seemed crazy but I had to try it anyway before I would call the on-call resident to help. The patient laid on his back on the floor. I sat facing him on the floor also, after taking my shoes off. I stretched out my left foot into his left armpit while pulling his arm with all my strength. After a while I could feel his muscles relax from exhaustion. I was exhausted, too. We immediately got up from the floor. I had maneuvered his arm back into place. He was so grateful. For myself, I was tremendously relieved and felt good that my studies had brought forth fruit.

Another incident was an old lady who apparently yawned too much. Her jaw was dislocated and her mouth was wide open. She was in obvious agony with tears in her eyes and soft sounds coming from her throat as if begging for a miracle. The women who brought her were all dressed in long black attire, common among the poor and a must for widows for the rest of their lives. Some were crying and asked me to help. However, I could not remember the sequence of the maneuvering of the jaw and I didn't want to do any harm. Fortunately, I found an appropriate book on a shelf in the emergency room. I read that section and within five minutes I began working on the old woman's jaw. After a few attempts the lower jaw snapped back into position.

There was obvious joy in the room, including my own. The shrill cry of jubilation commonly uttered during weddings and happy occasions filled the air when the women vibrated their tongues, producing a sound like no other and perfected by Egyptian women. I wanted to check if my patient could open and close her mouth normally. She refused to do so for fear it would happen again. On the urging of her friends, however, she opened her mouth slightly and closed it again. It was, to all concerned including me, a miracle.

Many patients came to the E.R. with severe renal colic. Surgery for kidney stones had very high morbidity and complications. Many patients preferred a symptomatic treatment with pain killers during the attacks. The usual treatment was a shot of morphine. There were no obvious signs of a kidney stone that a doctor could test for in the clinic. So he had to depend on the level of the patient's screams. It was difficult to be sure if a man had a stone or was a drug addict. Some of them knew this, and came in usually after midnight for a fix, rotating between various hospitals in the city and offering different body sites for the injection each time.

It was easier for us to give them the shot and get it over with. One night a man came in with these symptoms. For his bad luck I had the resident physician checking another patient. Apparently that physician knew Ali from the previous year.

The doctor said to him, "Ali, if you still have that kidney stone since last year, you need surgery."

Ali responded, "I am afraid of surgery. The shot is all I need."

The devious resident physician gave Ali a 1cc injection of pure alcohol under the skin. Ali came in several nights later with a deep ulcer the size of a penny, and was in real pain. I learned what an alcohol injection can do. There was no such thing as malpractice litigation in Egypt at that time.

The next rotation was general surgery. For an intern it was the hardest rotation. The word "slave" does not adequately describe it. Surgeons think they are gods. In their hands they hold a scalpel and literally the life of the patient. The most tiring job was in the operating room. The surgeon and his assistant performed the surgery. To keep the abdominal cavity or whatever part of the body open for the surgeons to work on we used retractors, especially for gall bladder surgery. The intern had to hold on to the metal retractor gently with an outstretched arm, often standing behind the surgeon at an angle. The pull on the retractor had to be strong enough to keep the abdomen open and gentle enough not to tear the liver.

After half an hour our arms would be tired, but we had to endure. One such operation for neck cancer took eight hours. At lunch time, a nurse brought a milk shake with a straw close to my face, uncovered my face mask and shoved the straw into my mouth as my two hands were not free. It was an awkward meal, but kept me from fainting. Every now and then the surgeon would move a little and show the intern what he had done. It was interesting but not very educational from a practical point of view.

One incident left a lasting impression on me in a negative way. A well-known surgeon who was a chain smoker was also notorious for his utmost rudeness. He would keep his cigarette still in his mouth as he entered the operating room, despite the sign that said, "No Smoking." The nurses were scared of him.

Each surgeon had two mornings or two afternoons a week in the operating room. He would line up his patients and start at 7 a.m. Other patients followed as time permitted. In the afternoons he went to his private practice office where he could make a lot of money. One day some surgeries took longer than expected. The surgeon had to leave to go to his private practice clinic. One patient, an elderly man from the countryside, had come in for a free hemorrhoid surgery. He was told by that surgeon at noon that the surgery was to be postponed for two days. The man was upset, especially when he had gone through the unpleasant preparation of multiple enemas necessary for the procedure.

The surgeon angrily told the elderly man, "You may get a full refund for the zero money you paid."

The man tried to argue. The surgeon, in a rage, slapped the patient's face. I was stunned. I have never forgotten it and it still makes me shudder.

Interns were allowed to do minor surgery outside the abdomen. These included draining breast abscesses in women, varicocele in the scrotum of men, and simple hernias. I did a varicocele surgery for a middle-aged man, cutting and tying the swollen and tortuous veins.

We usually sent the surgical specimens to the pathology lab for tissue identification and microscopic evaluation. A few days later the pathology report arrived stating that there was also a small section of the vas deferens, which is the narrow tube that carries the sperm out of the testicle. In essence, I had inadvertently performed a vasectomy on the man. I was horrified. I was sure I had made the man infertile by my mistake. I expected a major reprimand or punishment. However, the surgical resident in charge of the case only reprimanded me mildly.

He said, as I was tearing up, "Don't take it too hard. God has given us two testicles. This man still has one, and even if he became infertile, he would be doing the overpopulated country a favor!"

One of the interesting surgeries was a man in his twenties who came from Upper Egypt, some three hundred miles away, for circumcision. Apparently all the men in his family had to be circumcised, as were most small boys in all religions, Muslims, Christians and Jews. For Jews it was a sacred duty, for others it was a respected custom.

Somehow the patient had missed being circumcised as a boy, which was usually done in the first few months at home by the town's barber. Now, the man was going to get married and wanted to get circumcised in a Cairo hospital far away from home. He told his family he was going on a business trip. He knew one resident physician in our hospital who had been his hometown friend many years earlier and who facilitated the unusual admission. The man was taken to the operating room for the brief surgery at the end of the day. It was decided that it would be done under general anesthesia to avoid embarrassment.

During the induction of anesthesia, just prior to the patient becoming unconscious, some men have a brief erection. During surgical procedures on the abdomen, chest or other parts of the body, the genitals were usually under the sheets and no one noticed. But this man's genitals were quite a sight. As he inhaled the gas, his penis started to swell. It was exposed for all to see. It finally stood up with its glistening head pointing to the overhead spotlight. It must have been ten inches long! The doctor called the nurses to come and see the awesome sight before it went down. Several came over. There was giggling and jokes all around. Fortunately, the man was out and never knew what a commotion he had caused.

Despite all of the muscle aches, the heartache, and the headaches during those three months of rotation, I learned a great deal. Advanced cancer and the variety of pathology I saw were enormous. It was an excellent educational experience to correlate symptoms and signs of diseases with what the diseased organs looked like in a living body.

Other rotations were much shorter and often overlapped, or were simultaneous, one in the morning and a different one in the afternoon. One such rotation was the burn ward. It was one of the most awful rotations. Many cases were there for months. Almost all had infected wounds and most were young people. Each story was tragic in a way. Very few were caused by a burning house. The two most common causes were attempted suicide following a broken love relationship, mostly girls, and the other was a failure in school, especially the dreaded high school exam for boys. They'd pour kerosene over their clothes and then light a match. Many, of course, died, but those who survived were referred to the University Hospital. The ward smelled of putrefied skin and pus. The first day on that ward I was extremely nauseated and vomited all day long. I could not take it. Reading the charts and seeing those young people suffering was more than I could bear. Looking at the infected large areas of the body and smelling the most pungent smell one could imagine gave me the shivers. The hell with training. I simply couldn't take it. I paid one of the nurses some money to do the dressings for me during that awful one-week rotation.

Another one-week rotation that month was on the rabies ward. Cairo University Hospital was the only place for in-patient services for rabies. Stray dog bites were common. Many people in large cities received the necessary shots locally in doctors' offices, but those in the countryside had to come to Cairo for the fourteen days of daily injections. It was an easy job for me but hard on the patients. Those long needles given under the abdominal wall must have been very painful. Thankfully, no one developed rabies or died on that ward during my rotation.

Orthopedics was also on our rotation schedule. It was rewarding both for the patients and myself. Mending broken bones, performing surgery on torn ligaments, and suctioning fluid from a swollen knee were greatly appreciated by the patients. However, the tools orthopedic surgeons used were a cross between carpentry and butchery: knives, hammers, nails, screws and glue. It was crude. There were no knee or hip replacements, and back surgery results were not great. I learned to put a cast on properly on fractured bones but the scariest part was taking the cast off after the bone healed. We used electric saws and had to be very careful to cut only the cast and not the skin under it as there were no safety blades back then. We were as fearful as the patients. Thankfully I never cut any skin.

A crazy one week rotation was to assess the safety and appropriateness of the food from the suppliers every morning. It was an easy job. We knew the signs of bad meat, bad fruit or bad milk. An interesting one was the eggs. When we put a few eggs in a pot with water and a certain amount of salt, the eggs should sink. If they floated they were spoiled and rejected. We also checked to see if the watermelon was ripe by opening some of the one hundred fruits to be sure they were ripe but not over-ripe. The supplier used to open two or three watermelons for us and they were usually good. It seemed that he knew what he was doing and picked the right ones. I asked him one day if I could pick which watermelon was opened to be tested. He said, "Okay."

I was an expert in this from my Beni Suef days. Patting the large fruit with a hand, like a drum, produces different sounds depending on the fruit being under-ripe, ripe, and over-ripe. I picked out one that was obviously under-ripe. I was correct. Then I picked one which I thought was over-ripe. It was. Usually the supplier doesn't count the undesirable watermelons that had been cut open, and the intern signs for the rest. I was unhappy and asked him to open many more watermelons.

He was mad when I told him I would not sign until I was satisfied. He balked and went to the hospital supply section chief. The chief called me into his office.

"What do you think you're doing?" he demanded.

"Sir, I am concerned that not all of the fruit is ripe."

Nevertheless, he signed the papers and said, "Well, if we don't accept the produce there will be no time left today to buy any from the local fruit stores. The patients will miss out."

I was mad, but didn't want to cause problems for the hospital. An hour later the chief called me into his office again. He'd thought of something else. Interns were allowed one week vacation during the year if their supervisor approved. Very few interns actually took that vacation.

"How many days are still owing you from that one week rotation?" he asked.

"Three," I replied.

"Do you need a three-day vacation?"

"Yes!" I said quickly.

The author, fourth from left middle row, stands next to a professor with other students on the rooftop of the university hospital on a branch of the NileRiver in Cairo.

He immediately handed me a piece of paper for requesting a vacation. I filled it out and he signed it. I took three days off and enjoyed myself. I avoided further confrontations but I think there must have been kickbacks between the chief and the supplier.

One interesting rotation was skin and venereal diseases. I don't know what combined the two but it was probably because syphilis gave sufferers a skin rash in its secondary phase. This was before the development of penicillin for the treatment of many venereal diseases. The specialist was able to distinguish syphilis rash from other skin rashes for appropriate treatments. The professors were so good that they would diagnose patients within a few minutes of a brief history-taking and a brief physical examination. We saw a multitude of skin rashes and diseases.

There was one weekly clinic for chronic prostatitis. In those cases antibiotics were supplanted by intra-rectal massage of the prostate to drain as much as possible of the infected material which drips from the penis. I was not good at it. My index finger is short, so the rectal massage was not very productive. Many of our patients came regularly. They preferred one exceptionally tall intern who had long fingers. One man who seemed effeminate said that he liked that doctor because the longer fingers gave him comfort. I presumed that it was more than medical comfort. The word spread that I was not good at it. Some patients refused to let me do the prostatic massage, saying that I was not experienced enough. No problem. I took the rest of the day off.

One intern developed jaundice. He became very tired, lost weight and had to take a few weeks off. In retrospect I'm sure he had hepatitis B, usually contracted from a needle after drawing blood or giving an intravenous injection to a patient who carried that virus. Fortunately the intern recovered completely and continued his training.

Many interns had more money to spend than ever before. Almost all were single and in their twenties. Occasionally they went downtown to have sex with prostitutes. Somehow, one of the interns arranged with a janitor to bring a prostitute to the interns' quarters for one night and asked several of them to share the cost and delights. They used a room whose occupants were away. Each participant had half an hour with her. I guess it was convenient for everybody but the word spread and the hospital administration reprimanded the interns and fired the janitor. It never happened again.

As the training year came to a close, most interns already had a plan in motion for the following year. Several were going to work for the Armed Forces, which was considered glamorous in those days under President Nasser. Others had government jobs, mostly in the countryside. Some graduates were pursuing residency training in a specialty, and a few went to join their fathers who were physicians in private practice.

Ten were planning to go to America for further training.

I was one of them.

Chapter 22
PREPARING FOR AMERICA

One of my dreams in childhood was to visit other countries, especially America, and see in reality what I saw in the movies, but with our limited means it was unrealistic. No one from our family went abroad except my rich uncle who went to Europe every summer with his French wife and two boys. Then, a number of things happened in 1956 and 1957 that made that dream not so farfetched after all.

President Gamel Abdel Nasser of Egypt proposed building a dam near the southern city of Aswan to avoid losing water from the Nile during the flood season that occurred every summer to the Mediterranean Sea. A dam would have cost an enormous amount of money so he asked America for help. They wanted to do a feasibility study to look into the viability, impact and cost of the project but this would have taken a few years. Nasser was impatient. He wanted to start right away. In addition, the American Secretary of State, John Foster Dulles, included some conditions which Nasser considered unacceptable.

America's assistance was turned down. Nasser, furious at being spurned, turned to the Soviet Union's premier, Nikita Khrushchev, to step in. The Cold War was at its height in 1956. He promised to help. From that time on, Nasser considered Russia a friend and the USA an enemy.

At the same time Nasser was negotiating with Britain and France about the lease of the Suez Canal which was built in 1866. The two European countries, through a private company, were to run it for ninety-nine years, sharing its income with Egypt. Britain and France wanted to extend the lease; Nasser wanted to cut it short. The lease would have expired in 1965. The three reached an impasse. Nasser wanted hard currency income for his projects and adventures in Africa and the Middle East.

His next step was to unilaterally nationalize the Suez Canal in July 1956. Tensions developed. Negotiations failed. Through his fiery speeches and preparation for war, tension escalated. In October 1956, Britain, France and Israel seized the Suez Canal. He asked the Security Council to intervene.

It was bad timing for America. Russia had just crushed a revolution in Budapest, Hungary, and Khrushchev was now threatening to send missiles to Western Europe if America intervened. At the same time, the U.S. was in the middle of a presidential election. President Eisenhower was upset with Britain and France as they apparently didn't consult with him prior to the attack and seizure of the canal. He backed a resolution of the Security Council in the United Nations to demand a cease-fire and withdrawal of the three invading countries.

Eisenhower won re-election but Nasser was not grateful for his support. Instead, he declared that Egypt won the war over three countries. All the newspapers and the only radio station in Egypt were controlled by the government.

Hatred of all foreigners reached a feverish pitch, especially towards Jewish people living in Egypt. Their properties were seized and those who didn't have Egyptian citizenship, which included many Europeans, were threatened with expulsion. There was an exodus of Greeks, Italians, Armenians and Jews. Many were owners of large department stores and jewelry stores but they were forced to leave in haste with very little money. Nasser became the hero of the Arab world. They considered him the new Sallahuddin, a brilliant Muslim leader who defeated the crusaders in the twelfth century.

In the middle of all this turmoil, I was a junior in the medical school. We were ordered to volunteer for the Medical Corps. The universities were closed. My father was reluctant to see his prize son go to a war zone where I might be killed. To no avail. We were told that those who didn't volunteer would be punished and may never graduate. I had no choice but to join the Army Medical Corps. We were sent to a barrack outside of Cairo, given officer's uniforms and took twenty-four hour shifts waiting for casualties. Remarkably, none appeared. The war was over within two weeks. However, those two weeks gave me a glimpse of life in the army, and it was not pleasant, to say the least.

In 1957, a new cold war between Russia and America opened opportunities on the educational front. Both countries offered scholarships to students from third world countries for graduate studies at their universities. The goal was to teach, but also to indoctrinate those students who would be grateful to return to their countries, praising the affection for their host countries.

To this end, American hospitals offered many training positions for young doctors from around the world. They devised an exam in 1957, Educational Council for Foreign Medical Graduates (ECFMG), which tested both knowledge in medicine and English language. The object was to protect the safety of American patients and maximize the possibility for success of the foreign trainees to achieve their goal.

Nasser wanted to emulate the Soviet system in many ways. Egypt's Secret Service was implanted in every street. Large meetings were forbidden. Those who objected to any government policy were taken in the early morning hours to police stations for interrogation. Many never returned. Desert camps in Egypt for dissenters simulated those in Siberia. So the idea of going to America for training became appealing, although I didn't know how to go about it.

Enter Father Makary El Soriany, a Coptic Orthodox monk who had returned from America, having received a Master's degree in Christian Education from Princeton University in 1955. Atef, a close friend of mine since grade school in Beni Suef, and I went to Father Makary for advice. He encouraged us to go to the USA and said he'd try to facilitate our adventure. He also said that the famous Coptic Hospital in Cairo was manned and run by old Coptic physicians and surgeons and that if we were American trained, we would be qualified to take over that hospital.

We were thrilled. He wrote to Dr. Forman, one of his contacts at the National Council of Churches in the United States. Within a few weeks, early in 1958, as we were just beginning our internships at Cairo University Hospital, we received correspondence from Dr. Forman with the names and application forms for several hospitals in New York City and New Jersey who were advertising for interns in various medical journals. How excited we were at this turn of events!

146

We subsequently met with Father Makary on many occasions. He helped us fill out the applications, told us how to correspond with these hospitals, corrected our English, and always inquired about our progress. Two years earlier he had done the same with a physician named Salama who went to New York City for pediatric residency. Two other new graduates also received help from Father Makary in obtaining scholarships. One went to study for a Master's degree in History in Chicago, while the other studied for a Master's degree in Christian Education in Connecticut. These three people were very helpful to us later on.

In October 1958, we received good news: Our applications had been reviewed for acceptance the following July, pending receipt of two letters of recommendation, one for academic and one a personal reference. Father Makary wrote the personal reference for us. No professor at the medical school wanted to write an academic reference. One of them, with whom I worked in the Internal Medicine Department, said plainly, "All letters are opened by the Censorship Section of the Post Office. They would question me as to why I am corresponding with an enemy country, the USA. They might put my name on their blacklist."

I was shocked but understood his dilemma as being put on a blacklist would doom a person from promotion or leaving the country and may put him under continuous surveillance. In despair, I went to Father Makary once again and asked for his guidance. He contacted a Christian physician who worked in the Department of Physiology. She wrote a nice letter of recommendation for me. Another hurdle thankfully was overcome.

In early December 1958, I received a letter from Saint Barnabas Medical Center in Newark, New Jersey, stating:

"You have been accepted for a rotating internship position starting July 1st, 1959. Your stipend will be $100 per month plus room and board in the interns' quarters on hospital grounds. We look forward to your arrival. If we can be of help, please let us know."

Greatly elated, I visited Father Makary once more. He told me that I needed two things: an entry visa to the USA and an exit visa from Egypt. At that time, no one could leave Egypt without a permit to leave signed by the Minister of Interior or his deputy. I filled out the required forms.

The American part went smoothly. In February 1959, I received a letter requesting me to appear for an interview with the American Consul in Cairo. Before I went, I did some homework, studying the geography of New Jersey and American government, not knowing what questions he might ask. On the designated day, I went to the American Consulate one hour early. I was pretty nervous.

I gave my name and showed the interview appointment letter to his secretary. To my surprise, he came out within a few minutes, shook my hand and invited me into his office. The consul was tall and handsome, just like the men in American movies. He asked me to sit down and relax. I showed him the letter of acceptance from the hospital in New Jersey. We chatted for a few minutes. He had an accent different from our British trained professors. Occasionally, I didn't get what he was saying but I nodded my head periodically as if I understood.

He asked me why I picked Newark, New Jersey. I actually had no idea about the city, only the state. I didn't reveal that it was the only hospital that sent me an acceptance letter. Instead, I told him I liked it because it was close to New York City with its many attractions. He was obviously pleased that I had some knowledge of the area.

At the end of the interview he said that I needed a physical examination, some lab tests, and a chest x-ray to complete my application. He gave me the name of two physicians in Cairo who dealt extensively with the American Consulate. A month later, all my papers were complete. I took the reports in a sealed envelope from one of the physicians and gave them to the Consul's secretary. She said that everything seemed in order and that the visa would be stamped on my Egyptian passport when I got one. I was halfway there!

The Egyptian side, not surprisingly, was another story, considering the bureaucratic government. For over a month I did not receive even an acknowledgement that anything was in progress. I returned to consult with Father Makary in late February. He told me he would contact some government officials to speed up the process. He was well liked and well connected because he had supported the Palestinians' rights in an ecumenical meeting, endearing Father Makary to the Egyptian government. He also told me to be in the USA before June 10th, as there was a conference in Chicago about missionary work in third world countries organized by the National Council of Churches in America and that he would not be able to go. He asked if Atef and I would represent the Coptic Church and read his report to the conference. He also said that we would be their guests, so they would pay all our expenses during the three day conference including transportation from New York City and back. Another great experience in store for us!

148

We went to Thomas Cook, a well-known travel agency in Cairo, and informed the agent of our plan. We naturally asked for the least expensive way to travel to be in New York before June 10th. It became obvious that flying was out of the question as we had to pay extra for the luggage and I intended to take many medical school books, which alone weighed over sixty pounds as well as clothes and other things. So travel by sea was the way to go.

The travel agent found that the cheapest way would be to take a boat from Naples, Italy, across the Atlantic Ocean to New York. From Egypt, we would take a boat across the Mediterranean Sea from Alexandria to Naples. The best deal and best time was to leave Alexandria May 21st, reach Naples May 25th, take the transatlantic boat May 27th and arrive in New York June 4th. The cost was 100 Egyptian pounds or $260 including a train ticket from Naples to Rome and back, so we could spend time touring Rome. Excitedly, we made our reservations and paid the deposit.

It turned out that I needed clearances from various Egyptian agencies and ministries. Each had its own rules and paperwork. I quickly realized that each employee at these agencies had a small part such as reviewing an application for completeness, another for recording that it was received, a third was responsible for the agency stamp after several levels signed off. No employee was permitted to handle the job of another, so when one was sick or on vacation, the application would sit on his desk till he returned. It was bureaucracy at its worst. Clearances had to come from the taxation agency stating that I owed no taxes, from the Ministry of Health that I was not drafted to serve, from the Armed Service that I was not a draft dodger, and from the Secret Service that I was not on the government blacklist for unwanted political activity.

March and April were very stressful. I shuttled from one agency to another to find out where my papers were, at least to be sure that they were not lost. Each employee spoke nicely but also said that they had to follow proper procedure. What a nightmare! I knew that I was not going to be drafted, I knew that I owed no taxes, but I didn't know if I was on any blacklist.

One day a Secret Service agent arrived at our apartment. Apparently he was collecting information about me from neighbors, other college students, the grocery store clerks down the street, and probably others. I knew about him because one of the grocery employees told me about being asked if I was involved in any suspicious activity and whether I left or came home at odd hours. The Secret Service agent wanted to know from him who my friends were as well as any involvement in community activities. Obviously, according to him, I was clear.

The agent was a man in his forties, wearing a long flowing white galabia. He asked me why I was going to a non-friendly country and who my contacts were in America, and whether I voted for Nasser in the last election. I told him I was going because the medical training was excellent in America, that it would not cost Egypt any money, and that I would represent Egypt by telling American people about our great country and its accomplishments, past and present.

Father Makary gave me fifty or so 35mm color slides about ancient and modern Egypt to help with any presentations, as foreign students were often invited to speak locally in America. I showed the color slides to the agent. He was impressed. After drinking the Coca-Cola I offered him, he asked me if I had any medication samples for a cough as his son was sick. As an intern we saw many drug companies' representatives who gave us samples for our own use. I told him I had, and gave him several bottles. He was happy, shook my hand and left.

Obviously I passed, but it took another whole month for the security clearance to be signed at so many levels in the Department of the Interior. I know because I visited various offices on a weekly basis to see where my papers were. Periodically I got anxious wondering if the paperwork would be finished in time for the May 21st sailing. At other times, I got miserably depressed wondering if I would ever leave Egypt. I lost six pounds from March to May, down to 118 pounds.

Money was another issue. I was able to save only 30 pounds during my internship. Even though my father gave me 50 pounds, it was not enough. I needed another 50 pounds ($130) to pay for the ticket balance and to exchange 20 pounds to foreign currency which was the maximum allowed by the government for those who wanted to leave the country. That rule, of course, was designed to keep hard currency in Egypt, but also prevented Egyptians from traveling abroad. What to do? I went to my uncles and aunts asking for help. They gave me the needed money and more. I was extremely grateful for their generosity.

May 14th was a red letter day. I received every single clearance I needed. The next step was to get a passport, an exit visa from Egypt, and entry visas for the USA and Italy. Employees at the only Egyptian passport office in downtown Cairo were grumpy and envious. They issued passports to those who wanted to leave the country, while they themselves could not. It was a feeling many had that Egypt was a very large prison.

The information to be filled out on the application form included date and place of birth, job classification, and religion. Christians and Jews were given a hard time if the passport employee was a fanatical Muslim, and an easier time if the employee was a Christian. Not that the passport would be denied but the delay and treatment one received was biased that way. It was too easy to tell an applicant that the employee who had the stamp was sick and you needed to come back tomorrow or the day after. They could be nice or rude for no obvious reason.

Luckily for me, it so happened that my older brother, Philip, knew someone who worked in the passport office. It was a God-given gift. I could breathe again! He facilitated the process, which took a mere two days. They wrote on the passport the name of the countries I was allowed to visit one by one. There was no such thing as a passport with unlimited permission to visit all countries. Of course, they had to include the USA, as that was my destination, but they had to see the travel ticket in order to add Italy as I was going to visit it for two days before we'd sail from there.

The next day, I ran to the U.S. Consulate. They stamped the entry visa and gave me the sealed envelope with my medical report and x-ray. I then ran all the way to the Italian Consulate, showed them the passport and the tickets, including the train ticket between Rome and Naples. They took them, asked for the fee, and told me to come the next day. I was exasperated. I tried to argue my urgency. No luck. That was their procedure and they were sticking with it. It was now May 18th. The boat would leave three days later. Sleepless nights ensued, stress, and physical upheaval.

Another issue was that no books or any printed material was to leave Egypt without first being inspected by the censor's office. I was planning to take most of my medical books, a bible, and some spiritual books. My father bought three large suitcases made of cow's hide, real leather. Each weighed ten pounds when empty, but they were very sturdy. I put all the books in one suitcase. It weighed sixty pounds. I could hardly lift it. My father was able to, though. We went together to the main post office downtown Cairo to the Publication Censor's office. The employee was professional but wanted to be sure that there were no anti-government publications in the suitcase. He frowned when he saw my Bible, but didn't say anything. Finally he put red tape around the suitcase with government stamps at strategic locations. We were tremendously relieved and took the suitcase back home. I felt bad for my sixty-three-year old father carrying it up three flights in our house, but with my small, 118-pound frame, there was no way I could do it.

My saga continued. The next stop was to go to the Foreign Exchange office with the passport and money. It happened that the head of that office in Cairo was originally from Beni Suef and from a prominent Christian family. Another stroke of good luck! The maximum money allowed out of the country was 20 pounds, the equivalent of $52. I chose $42 in U.S. currency and $10 in Italian currency for our two-day stay there in Italy. This amounted to 8,000 lire.

On May 19th, everything was finally ready for my great adventure to the new world. What an incredible relief after all the frustrations, although I was not entirely free from stress as I was to leave Cairo the next day, May 20th, in order to board the boat from Alexandria to Naples on May 21st.

May 19th was a hectic day. The three large suitcases were ready. One was heavily padlocked, red taped, and book-filled, another had most of the clothes I owned including wool suits, a heavy coat, and a plethora of Egyptian cotton shirts and underwear. The third suitcase included many souvenirs and Egyptian antiques that my father, unselfish as ever, said that I could sell if I needed money upon arrival in the USA or to give as presents to those that helped me. Friends and relatives came to the house all day and into the night to bid farewell to the first person to go to America from the family or, in fact, the neighborhood. Everyone was as excited as I was. We eventually got to sleep at 2 a.m.

Chapter 23
VOYAGE TO AMERICA

The next morning we hauled the three suitcases to the main train station in Cairo. There were about thirty people bidding me farewell, mostly cousins and close friends, as well as my brothers and sisters. Only my parents and I boarded the train for the three-hour trip to Alexandria. We were met by my sister who was attending the College of Pharmacy in Alexandria University. We arrived at 4 p.m. and went to a hotel for the night. The next morning we went to the pier to board the Greek ship, the *Messalia.*

There were four classes on the Mediterranean ship compared to three on the transoceanic ship which had first, second, and third class accommodations only. Our ship had a fourth class called "deck" which meant no cabin. Travelers on deck were almost always male students or workers going to Europe for the summer, looking for jobs. They brought their own food and used public bathrooms on the ship. They had sleeping bags and slept under the stars. There was no rain during the summers except inland in Europe. Our tickets were third class, so beds and food were included in our fare. However, my mother and my friend Atef's mother felt that we might not like the ship's food so they packed sandwiches, cheeses, meat, pastries, boiled eggs, and bread for us.

It took more than two hours to get on the ship, from noon to 2 p.m. It was an emotional farewell. My father tried to control the tears in his eyes. My mother didn't want to let go of me. She gave me the longest hug, crying and saying "Will I ever see you again before I die?" I cried, too. After we boarded we were directed to our cabin. It was near the bottom of the ship with double bunk beds for four people and no windows or washing facilities. The sinks, bathrooms and showers were down the hallway. We found that the other cabin mates were Jordanians who lived in America and were returning from visiting their families. Back on deck, we saw our families on the shore waving and crying.

The boat left at 5 p.m. As it started moving, the crying got louder and more intense, especially from my mother. It was sad but my inner excitement was almost uncontrollable. Gradually people on shore became smaller and smaller as the ship headed out and we could only see a myriad of handkerchiefs from the hundreds of travelers' families waving. Finally, we lost sight of the mainland and were at sea.

Atef and I chose the early meal seating. A bell rang at 6 p.m. for dinner. We went to the dining room where there were long tables for self-seating. The food was unbelievable: Greek delicacies, several kinds of meat, vegetables, fruits and desserts that we were not used to at home. No need of mom's food that she'd packed for me. We were happily stuffed. Neither Atef nor I had any drinks, however, as we had to pay for them. In Egypt, we only drank beer or wine at home on special occasions. It was not a weekly affair.

In fact, we bought nothing on the ship in order to save our small amount of money for essentials. As we went up to the deck after eating dinner, the sun was starting to set over the horizon. It was a beautiful sight not seen in crowded Cairo with its high rise buildings everywhere.

To our pleasant surprise, the young people on deck were a fun-loving, music-playing bunch. They had flutes, drums, ouds (similar to a guitar), accordions and violins. They were from Egypt, Lebanon, Syria and Jordan. The best Arabic songs and music at that time came from Egypt and we joined them in singing until midnight. Under a clear sky and a nice breeze we all had fun. We went down to sleep while they continued on deck until God-knows-when. I chose the upper bunk and Atef, the lower. The two youths from Jordan took the other two beds. One of them was a door-to-door salesman in Indiana. He told us some wild stories about his job and how he stayed overnight sometimes in a farmer's house, and his adventures with girls. I don't know if he was making stories up or not, but he surely was very entertaining. The other guy was quiet.

On the morning of May 23rd we arrived at Piraeus, the main Greek port not far from Athens. We were told that a bus would leave the ship after breakfast en route to Athens. Those who wanted to go to town could take the bus back to the ship at 3 p.m. I exchanged $2 for 60 drachmas. The bus dropped us near the Acropolis. We could only look at it from the outside as admission tickets were beyond our means. We had just enough money for a few postcards, stamps, lemonade and apples, which comprised our lunch.

We wrote to our families and mailed the cards. Then we visited a museum for free and were headed back to the place where the bus would pick us up when suddenly the sky became dark and a heavy rain began to fall as if someone had opened a faucet in the sky. We were not used to such an event; no coat, no umbrellas. We huddled next to a house. Someone came out and invited us in until the rain stopped. They spoke no English. We spoke no Greek. We were afraid we'd miss the bus when suddenly, to our surprise, after ten minutes the rain stopped and the sun came out. What crazy weather! We made our way back to the *Messalia*.

It was good to be spending another day at sea. The food and entertainment were both exceptional. At night there was music and dancing. We watched for a while, but we preferred the boys on the deck where we could join in Arabic singing. When we got back to the room we smelled something rotten. The culprit was our packed food, of course. It was vile. Because of our busy activities on board we'd forgotten about the food my mother had given us for the trip. We took it up to the deck in a hurry so no one would see or smell it and threw it to the fish. I never told my mother that her labor of love was in vain. We left the windowless cabin door open for air and the smell gradually decreased. Fortunately for us, our two cabin companions were on deck all day and only came to the cabin after midnight.

On the morning of May 25th, the *Masselia* arrived at Naples, its final destination. Everyone had to disembark with their luggage. We were told that we could store it at the port for 65 liras per suitcase per day. The price was certainly reasonable, but how were we to carry those six heavy suitcases (three each for Atef and me)? To our pleasant surprise, we heard our names on a loudspeaker telling us to meet a Thomas Cook Travel Agency representative. He said he would take our luggage to storage and to give him our tickets for the transoceanic boat, so that he could get us the boarding passes.

We were told in Egypt that there were many thieves in Italy and to be wary. If our suitcases were stolen we would be in big, big trouble so we walked with him to be sure the suitcases actually went to the storage place and hesitantly gave him the next boat's tickets.

Youssef, one of our Jordanian cabin mates, said he was going to Rome, also. We already had the tickets for the three-hour train ride. The views along the way were amazing. There were houses built on hills, over many levels. The mountains were all green with trees, something we had not seen in Egypt because of our lack of rain. Our only water came from the River Nile. Atef and I asked Youssef how they irrigated all those hills. He laughed and told us that it rained so frequently that they didn't have to pump water upward.

We told him how much money we had and asked if he knew of a very cheap hotel for two nights. We had $10 worth of liras each and wanted to keep some for the stored bags. Youssef found a hotel near the train station, a room with three single beds that cost 1,000 lira ($1.25) per night. We were really pleased and thanked him profusely. He also told us which bus to take to important landmarks in Rome. Youssef was truly heaven sent.

We visited the Vatican, several museums and the Coliseum. We were fascinated by all those statues, fountains and monuments. Unfortunately, we had no camera. We couldn't afford to buy any souvenirs, either, only a few postcards and stamps to send to our families. While in Rome we made our own sandwiches, as a sit-down restaurant was beyond our means. Street vendors sold watermelon by the piece, which we'd never seen in Egypt. One man was selling Parker fountain pens for $1. That was amazing to us as in Egypt they cost $5. On closer inspection, however, the logo on the pens was printed as "P.Arker." He was a really deceptive salesman that confirmed the stories of unscrupulous salesmen in Italy.

On May 27th, we woke up at 4 a.m. and took the 6 a.m. train back to Naples. We retrieved our luggage and received our boarding passes from the agent. We were grateful and gave him whatever liras we had left over as we had no need for them anymore.

The ship was magnificent and was named Christopher Columbus, a perfect name for new adventurers to the new world. At that time there were about ten large transoceanic ships in Europe. Two from Britain, namely the Queen Mary and the Queen Elizabeth, two from Italy, the Christopher Columbus and the Leonardo DaVinci, one from France named France, one from Holland called Amsterdam, one from Germany, and probably a few others whose names I don't remember.

Our ship was like a floating city. It was eight stories high, with a swimming pool, large restaurants, dance halls and other amenities, some of which were out of bounds for us third class passengers. Our cabin, we were happy to see, had only two single beds, but the shower and toilets were still down the hall. There was no deck class. We were told there were over a thousand passengers. The ship started moving late afternoon.

A small orchestra played on shore. Everyone on the ship, as well as their friends and relatives on shore, waved to each other, probably with the same emotional display the Italians are known for, as we had experienced in Alexandria. But this time Atef and I were not part of it.

The author, seated far left, and his friend, Atef, far right, and two Italian companions on the Christopher Columbus, making their way to America on June 2, 1959.

For two days we saw no land. The entertainment for third class passengers was not that great. A man played the piano all day while some people danced occasionally. I opened my sealed suitcase, got out some medical books, and spent time studying. I knew that I had to take the ECFMG exam in September and that I could get into a good residency training program the following year, but only if I passed.

The first two days I was lost a few times trying to find our cabin or the dining room. Each table seated four people. Our companions were two Italians living in America, a man in his forties who said he was a bartender, and the other in his thirties, who was always flirting with the women. The food was great and plentiful, even more than on the Greek ship. We had a menu to choose from. There was meat at every meal, something we were not used to. I watched what the Italian fellows ordered for breakfast: eggs and steak. Other days included ham and pork. We feasted every day and I gained four pounds from what I had lost during the last hectic two months in Egypt.

On the morning of May 30th, the ship stopped briefly at Gibraltar. We were told that we could get off for a few hours, which we did, again spending $1 buying post cards and British stamps and sending them off to Egypt. We spent a few more days in the Atlantic with the same routine, food and books. A day and a half before we arrived in New York harbor, the ocean got rough, the boat swayed, and most people got seasick. The dining room at dinner time was almost empty. I was nauseated, too, and returned to the cabin without eating. By the next morning the weather returned to normal. We were told that we would arrive at 7 a.m. on June 4th.

The passengers were given two envelopes and told to put the recommended tips in them, $1 per passenger per day for the dining staff and the same amount for the cabin crew. That meant $8 for each envelope. The envelopes were to be collected in the dining room at breakfast. That amount was almost half the money we had to our name. We decided to skip breakfast and avoid giving any tips.

Going down to check the cabin before disembarking, I met one of the waiters who served our table. Of course, he knew my reason for skipping breakfast. I felt ashamed, turned around and ran the other way. I could hear him cursing me in Italian which I neither understood, nor cared, but his tone of voice told it all. I had $38 in my pocket after spending $1 for a commemorative picture on the boat, $2 in Athens, and $1 in Gibraltar. The 800 lire had all been spent in Italy.

At 6 a.m. we went up on deck along with many others, watching the New York skyline in the distance. When the Statue of Liberty appeared, everybody clapped and cheered. I had tears in my eyes. I could hardly believe that my dream of coming to America had been realized.

"New York, here I come!"

Made in the USA
San Bernardino, CA
29 September 2018